REVENUE GR○WTH ENGINE

HOW TO ALIGN SALES & MARKETING TO ACCELERATE GROWTH

DARRELL AMY

Legal Disclaimer

Published by: Darrell Amy
ISBN: 978-1-7347743-1-3

Praise for Revenue Growth Engine

Sales and marketing alignment has been elusive for many companies. No longer! *Revenue Growth Engine* provides a framework of building outbound processes that drive exponential growth by attracting net-new clients and cross-selling more to current clients.

Jeb Blount, Author of *Fanatical Prospecting*

If you're not growing, you're not going anywhere. Right now, we need to rev that engine, put the pedal to the metal, and take off in order to drive and thrive. Darrell's book provides a game plan anyone can put into practice to experience a growth spurt that others can be jealous of and can emulate.

Jeffrey Hayzlett, Primetime TV & Podcast Host, Speaker, Author and Part-Time Cowboy

Finally, a book that calls out in a step-by-step manner what it takes to be successful in sales. Skip the fantasy talk, this is real talk from a sales leader who knows how to get it done, Darrell gives it to you straight and unfiltered. You don't read this book, you apply this book. Written by the leader who has done, it, Darrell Amy gives it to you straight and unfiltered.

Sales is about helping others see and achieve what they didn't think was possible and that's what this book will help you do. Written by a sales leader passionate about helping you achieve what you didn't think was possible, Darrell Amy breaks it all down for you. You can read a lot of books on sales but few do you read, learn, apply like you will with this book by Darrell Amy. The title says it all, Revenue Growth Engine.

Mark Hunter, Author of the bestsellers *A Mind For Sales*, *High Profit Prospecting*, and *High Profit Selling*

"Darrell Amy nails it! While I've always appreciated his big heart, straight talk, and authentic approach when it comes to sales, Darrell takes it to an entirely new level with Revenue Growth Engine where he tackles two of the biggest challenges sales leaders face today - aligning marketing and sales and executing an effective outbound attack to fill the top of the funnel. The principles in this book work every time they're deployed. Start reading and implementing and watch your pipeline swell and your sales soar!"

Mike Weinberg, Author of bestsellers *New Sales. Simplified.*, *Sales Management. Simplified.*, and *Sales Truth*

Sales and marketing are the growth engine of any company, but they're famous for operating in silos. Each with its own set of strategies and metrics driving their activities. But imagine if your sales and marketing efforts could be in lock-step, working together. All of those investments being optimized. That's where Darrell Amy comes in – he has created a complete playbook for anyone in sales, marketing, or entrepreneurship looking for smart, sustainable growth. *Revenue Growth Engine* will get you operating a new level. You'll amplify your growth, and you'll get to do that with your best clients.

Amy Franko, Author of *The Modern Seller* & *LinkedIn Top Sales Voice*

"Too many good businesses and hard-working professionals are frustrated. They can't seem to 'get it together'--whether that means aligning sales and marketing, or finding the right type of clients, or simply generating the level of growth that matches the value they offer to the world.

"If your team ever has difficulty getting it together, then this book is for you. Darrell Amy is both smart and generous. His approach is practical, proven, and one that might actually get your team re-energized for growth."

Jim Karrh, Author of *The Science of Customer Connections: Manage Your Message to Grow Your Business* **and host of** *The Manage Your Message Podcast*

"If you handle sales AND marketing – or who have teams that do – start a book club for this book. Read and discuss. In a few weeks time you could remove years of misunderstanding, miscommunication, and mistrust. It's the ideal way to have everything working together from beginning to end with a crystal-clear focus on the two ways to grow revenue as the foundation for it all. Great book!"

Andrea Waltz, Co-Author of *Go for No!*

Growing a business requires a plan, a process, and a strategic process. Darrell Amy has delivered a masterpiece! Preventative maintenance on your car keeps all cylinders firing for maximum performance.

Revenue Growth Engine provides a detailed roadmap on how to keep your business growth running on all cylinders. For a business to continue growing they must secure new business, increase their win rates, cross-sell to their clients and build client loyalty. With a servant's heart and mind, Darrell will guide you to profitable growth and a bright business future.

Larry Levine, Author of *Selling From the Heart*

When you need to rev up the Revenue Growth Engine of your business, read this book. Darrell Amy provides the understanding of what the critical focus points must be, why these matter so much, and how to put them into action - and make it work! *Revenue Growth Engine* will ignite your passion, drive your process in the right direction, and deliver the results to the finish line you want to cross. Pick it up and use it now.

Steve Lishansky, CEO, Optimize International, Author of *The Ultimate Sales Revolution - Sell Differently. Change the World*

"Darrell Amy is the real deal. Down to earth, fun, and innovative, Darrell brings together the things we love about our businesses and turns them into growth. *Revenue Growth Engine* is to be praised as an influential guide for those seeking Sales and Marketing alignment."

James Buckley, Director Sales Execution and Evolution, JB Sales

There are a lot of people who talk about the importance alignment, but only a few with the experience or the knowhow to show people how to put it all together. Darrell Amy is one of those people.

Maybe it's my Motor City roots, but I love the way Darrell uses the engine as an analogy for how all of the moving parts in the revenue-generating parts of an organization work together to move the whole thing forward. Engines are complex, but the one laid out in this book is much easier to understand. When you get done reading it, you'll have a much clearer idea of how to accelerate your revenues

Jeff Bajorek, *The Why and The Buy Podcast*

Darrell Amy, a proven leader with a track record of big wins showcases his secret playbook of how to grow revenue. The starting framework in the book "There are two ways to grow revenue. 1. You get more clients. 2. You sell more to your current clients." showcases the simplicity and having the eye on making a real impact. Unlike most business books, this needs no translation from academics to business tactics. Exciting, Energetic and Ready to use. A must-read as big revenue impact is inevitable.

Arjun Sen, Founder & CEO ZenMango

As has been my experience, Darrell intimately understands the power and the process of sales and marketing alignment/collaboration, and how to help companies leverage it to foster accelerated revenue growth. The Buyer's Journey is changing, and if you are not enlisting holistic sales + marketing know-how, the engine you use to drive growth will not produce peak performance. This book will certainly help!

Robert Caldwell, Vice President, Marketing, Datamax, Inc.

"Darrell has created a concise, integrated model to help business leaders to tackle the single most pressing concept for long-term business health: revenue growth. If revenue growth is the most important thing, then as business leaders we must take ownership of it and ensure it gets the necessary attention and resources in our companies. He ties together each of the core disciplines of sales and marketing and drives home the importance of a consistent, repeated message to both prospects and existing clients. This is a must-read for CEOs and business owners."

Adrian Chenault, CEO and Co-Founder, Contact Mapping

This book is a must-read for any business that wants a true system for growing revenue. *Revenue Growth Engine* goes in-depth into the roles of sales and marketing and how they work together to not only bring in new sales but also sell more to your current clients.

Darrell Amy demonstrates throughout the book his expertise and freely shares his knowledge.

Kim Thompson-Pinder, The Extraordinary Word Nina and Host of the *Author To Authority Podcast*

Ask yourself what's holding your organization back from the levels of growth you know should be possible with your products and services, and chances are you'll acknowledge that your current sales and marketing focus is not as well aligned as it could be.

In *Revenue Growth Engine*, Darrel Amy highlights the self-limiting gaps between sales and marketing efforts that exists for so many organisations, and simultaneously provides the vision and perspective needed to help organisations of any size become exceptional in the manner in which they serve and manage their current and prospective customer experiences, in order to truly accelerate their growth.

This book should be step 1 in the process for all business leadership and management team members involved with developing the revenue growth engine for your organisation.

Paul Brady, Founder & Managing Director / Business Enabled, Australia

OK, every business transaction has to do with someone selling something to someone. So does that happen by accident...well, rarely, but what IF you could become a master at the whole process and actually grow them. Actually grow your results? Darrell Amy has an amazing goal with this project, he wants to help YOU! With nearly 30 years in the sales trenches, I love how Darrell provides the "engine" for our success! This is a MUST read for everyone in sales!

Chris Gingrasso, Territory Sales Manager, US Floors

Want to accelerate your revenue growth? Think of your sales and marketing like an engine! If you aren't cruising at the speed you want, then you need to find where the misfire is, address it and start the engine again. Don't know where to start? Then, in this book, Darrell shows you how!

"All companies have some strategies in motion, but they are not aligned. Not only are they not supporting each other, but they are also pulling in different directions!"

To address this misalignment, Darrell identifies the parts of your Revenue Growth Engine (yep, prospecting is in there, but there's more to it than you think!), the fuel you need, and how to monitor your engine to keep it in peak performance. Remember, what doesn't get measured, doesn't change.

Darrell is very talented and knowledgeable. This is a great guide to get and keep your engine running smoothly!

Anna Scheller

Darrell Amy, in his book, *Revenue Growth Engine*, has given us "Formula #1" on how to successfully integrate marketing and sales into a fine-tuned, revenue producing business machine. Start your Engine, and ride with Darrell into a growing and profitable future.

Paul L. Barber, Retired - Former Vice-President of Sales & Marketing Precision Packaging Inc.

Resources

Free Tool Kit

Throughout the book, you will see helpful tools that you can download for free. To save you time, I've put them all on one page that you can access here:
www.RevenueGrowthEngine.net/free-tool-kit

Free Revenue Growth Engine Discovery Call

Would you like to get your team on the same page? Meet with one of our certified Revenue Growth Engine Implementers. Your team will get an overview of the Revenue Growth Engine framework along with examples of how companies similar to yours are growing. We will discuss your company goals. You'll learn about two ways that you can build your engine. Learn more here:
www.RevenueGrowthEngine.net/workshop

Book a Speaker

Would you like to motivate your audience to accelerate their revenue growth? Darrell Amy brings energy, excitement, and practical ideas to audiences of business owners, marketing professionals, and sales leaders. Learn more about how to book Darrell for your upcoming conference:
www.RevenueGrowthEngine.net/speaking

More Resources

If you have a great company, I want to help you grow. Here are some resources you'll find helpful. While you're on the website, make sure to sign up to get updates when we add new content.

- Revenue Growth Podcast:
  www.revenuegrowthpodcast.com

- Revenue Growth Blog:
  www.RevenueGrowthEngine.net/blog

- Favorite Revenue Growth Books:
  www.RevenueGrowthEngine.net/favorite-books

I dedicate this book to the great businesses that create meaningful jobs and give generously to their communities.

I want to help you grow so you can expand your impact!

Acknowledgments

Writing a book is a labor of love. As such, it takes a community of people cheering for you. Countless conversations with colleagues and clients blend with ideas from authors and podcasters to spark ideas. Out of this comes a book.

First, I want to thank my wife, Leslie. As the president of my fan club and my biggest cheerleader, she has given me a constant stream of encouragement.

This book wouldn't have happened without the inspiration of Larry Levine, my good friend and co-host of the *Selling From the Heart Podcast.* Larry's example of how to build a network around authenticity and how he works tirelessly to invest in that network has inspired me to do the same. I had a front-row seat to the journey he took in publishing the best-seller, *Selling From the Heart.* Now, Larry has been a co-pilot for me, guiding me through the publishing process.

A special thank you to Kim Thompson-Pinder, from RTI Publishing, my editor. Along with many hours, she has poured her heart into this book. Every step of the way, she offered encouragement and helpful insights.

Convergo, a growth strategy agency I founded in 2004, has given me a laboratory to test the ideas in this book. My talented team has not only been a sounding board for these ideas, but they have also built out the consulting model to help companies build and fine-tune their Revenue Growth

Engines. A huge thank you to Bill Poole, Lindsay Meade, Lisa Dalton, and the entire Convergo team, along with our open-minded clients.

I love new ideas. Every week, I am blessed to talk with leading sales, marketing, and business strategy thought leaders on the *Revenue Growth Podcast* and the *Selling From the Heart Podcast*. These conversations continue to form my growth philosophy, feeding my desire for innovation.

I am also grateful to the authors who have helped shape my thoughts. Jim Rohn famously said, "Formal education will make you a living; self-education will make you a fortune." The education I have received from the community of authors continues to make me a better person. So many authors have had a positive influence on my career. I want to specifically acknowledge Jay Abraham, Brent Adamson, Jeb Blount, Stephen Covey, Matt Dixon, Seth Godin, Tom Hopkins, Mark Hunter, Donald Miller, Tom Peters, Lee Salz, Marcus Sheridan, Mike Michalowicz, Gino Wickman, and many more. Books are the best source of education for any professional.

Three people have directly influenced my passion for helping businesses grow. Paul Barber, the co-chair of the Kingdom Missions Fund, has opened my eyes to the important role businesses play in funding critical non-profits. Scott MacGregor, founder of Something Good and the catalyst behind the book, *Standing O!* inspires me with his passion for using business as a platform for good things. Chris Gingrasso, the editor of *The W.O.W. Factor* book continues to motivate me to be a light in the marketplace.

Finally, I want to acknowledge Jesus Christ. Business and life present many challenges. He has walked with me on the mountaintops and carried me through the valleys. He has taught me how to love, the path of humility, and the importance of integrity. I owe my life to Him.

Table of Contents

xvii

Preface

S peaking at industry conferences has been a regular part of my career. However, this group was different. It was a mixed group of B2B marketing professionals, sales managers, and business owners, some of whom are former clients of mine.

Everyone in the crowd wanted to grow revenue, but they all had a different opinion as to what it would take to build.

Marketing managers were frustrated that others in the room did not see how buyers have changed. They wanted more buy-in from both sales and company management. They were hoping that the conference would be the tipping point for the executive team to go all-in on inbound marketing.

The room also included sales managers, most of whom, if they were honest, did not value marketing. They believed that the leads that came from marketing were soft and not useful to their team. Most of the sales managers felt that they needed more salespeople to prospect. One sales manager, who thankfully was not at the event, was so against marketing that he decided to bully his way to gutting the marketing budget so he could hire more sales reps.

The executives and business owners in the room were open-minded but confused as to how they should proceed. They wanted faster revenue growth, but simply plugging in a new marketing program seemed to be incomplete. Most had been down that road before and not seen results, so they were reluctant to dedicate budget.

What was worse, there was one company in the room that had gone all-in on inbound marketing. Their marketing director presented right before me, showing all the exciting new tactics and technologies. The marketing people were gaga, and the sales leaders were intrigued.

However, the truth serum came in the results. The prior year, the company had invested over $250,000 in two staff people, outside consultants, and technology. For their investment, they attributed $100,000 in sales revenue. Ouch.

Even with the lifetime revenue estimated at $500,000 for these clients, the industry typically ran 15 percent net profit. That meant that the investment of $250,000 yielded $75,000. Apparently, the Emperor had no clothes.

As I walked into the room to speak, the tension was not only palpable but one spark away from igniting. The inbound marketing believers were sitting at the front, eager to learn, while the skeptical sales managers sat in the back, only unfolding their arms to sip their black coffee.

What would I say to a group like this?

In the weeks leading up to the conference, our marketing agency team had done marketing and sales strategy reviews with both current and potential clients. They were making some investments in marketing and sales enablement but were expecting more growth than they were getting. Most of the clients have budgets for their website, social media, search engine optimization, and pay-per-click marketing. Some were fully committed to inbound marketing with marketing automation platforms and full certifications. Others were more old-school, sending marketing emails and doing events, having sales teams that were supposed to prospect, having CRMs, and access to prospect data.

Even with all this activity, new client growth rates were in the single digits. These businesses were also frustrated with the results of trying to sell additional services to existing clients.

These companies were disillusioned and disheartened, and it showed in their sporadic marketing and sales prospecting efforts. They certainly were not aligned.

That is when the light bulb moment happened!

I realized that the problem was not with inbound marketing, social media, pay-per-click advertising, or email open rates. It was not with sales prospecting and the debate over the death of the cold call in a world of social media.

The problem was bigger: there was no overall strategy. Marketing and sales tactics were not aligned. Most of all, they were not aiming at the primary goal: revenue growth.

At this moment, the idea of the Revenue Growth Engine emerged. Everything became apparent when I remembered that sales and marketing have the same objective: grow revenue.

Epiphany #1: There Are Only Two Ways to Grow Revenue

How do you grow revenue? There are two (and only two) ways to do it:

1. You get more clients.

2. You sell more to your current clients.

> There are two (and only two) ways to do it:
>
> 1. You get more clients.
>
> 2. You sell more to your current clients.

This may sound like an oversimplification. However, if you step back and look at your business, this makes sense. Furthermore, there is a good chance you are focused on only one of the two sources of revenue growth.

There are many ways to measure success in marketing and sales. That is the problem! When you have too many things to measure, everything becomes muddy.

Zoom out from the marketing and sales metrics to the primary goal of revenue growth, and two simple critical measurements of success come into focus:

Net-New Revenue. How many clients do we have?

Cross-Sell Revenue. What is the revenue per client? (A simple calculation: total revenue/number of clients.)

What if you could align your marketing and sales efforts around these two goals and metrics? What would it mean to revenue growth if you could show modest increases year after year in the number of clients and the revenue per client?

That is when I got out the calculator. I realized that if a company made small improvements in each of these two areas, it could create a powerful and sustainable pace of growth.

With a steady growth of 10–15 percent in each of these two areas, a company could double revenue in three years or less!

All the companies at the conference were growing. The problem was that they were only growing in one of the two areas. Like most companies, revenue growth focuses on the net-new business, with few seeing an increase in revenue per client.

That is when the lights came on. I opened a spreadsheet and started playing with numbers. If a company grew net-new business (number of clients) by 10 percent per year *and* cross-sell business (revenue per client) by 10 percent per year, they could double revenue in just over three years! If they averaged a 15 percent growth in each of these areas, it would take less than three years.

Double revenue! Organically? Is this possible? Yes!

Epiphany #2: Ideal Clients Accelerate Growth

Then the second epiphany happened: not all clients are created equal. Some are more valuable than others.

I began to remember The Pareto Principle. In the late 1800s, Vilfredo Pareto noticed that 20 percent of the people owned 80 percent of the land. He began to see this pattern throughout the economy. In most businesses, 20 percent of the clients generate 80 percent of the revenue and profits.

The key to accelerating growth was to focus on ideal clients. These are the type of clients that are candidates for cross-selling because they need everything that you sell. They are typically larger clients. They are also loyal clients.

If the business could attract and land more ideal clients, revenue would grow faster.

The problem is that most businesses are not optimized to attract ideal clients. Their sales teams are focused on quick wins with "bread and butter" clients. Of course, if you focus on these types of clients, you are going to be eating bread and butter.

To attract loyal clients, companies need to be intentional. They need a focused message that talks about the outcomes ideal clients want. They need sales and marketing processes to ensure that the ideal clients receive consistent coverage from marketing and sales.

With these epiphanies, I was able to speak at the conference with confidence. Instead of talking about marketing or sales tactics, I began with the real goal: growing revenue. We explored what it would take to develop net-new business and how companies could cross-sell additional services to their clients more effectively. With the goal of revenue growth, the marketing and sales enablement tactics started making sense.

Following the conference, I started reframing the way we talked to our clients. We kicked off our first Revenue Growth Workshop, where we set revenue goals based on the number of clients and revenue per client. We analyzed every aspect of the company's marketing and sales enablement efforts, identifying gaps, and low-hanging fruit. We established a plan that our clients could execute to fill in the gaps. Then, we committed to measuring results and moving above the noisy marketing data to hold ourselves accountable for the meaningful outcomes: the number of net-new business we added, and the revenue per client.

> Seeing revenue growth as the primary goal of sales and marketing brought everything into focus.

Seeing revenue growth as the primary goal of sales and marketing brought everything into focus.

I hope you have the same epiphanies as you read this book. Whether you are a digital marketing guru, an old-school sales leader, or a company owner, I hope you will see the forest through the trees. The Revenue Growth Engine is a guide to building an engine to drive exponential revenue growth with ideal clients.

The goal is simple: revenue growth. With this goal front and center, you will create a marketing and sales enablement strategy that drives more revenue than you may think is possible.

Why I am Passionate About Revenue Growth

I dedicate this book to great businesses and their leaders that are passionate about growing their business, doing remarkable work, taking care of their people, and making an impact in the community.

When good businesses grow, they amplify the impact of their work, making the earth a better place. They create excellent jobs in a world where most are stuck working for companies they do not like. Enjoyment in work leads to happier, financially stable families who give back, providing the lifeblood for much-needed non-profit organizations.

Small businesses create most jobs and are concerned about their employees. Large companies lay off employees with about the same emotional energy as taking out the trash. These vibrant small businesses need the tools to proliferate into robust and reliable medium-sized companies.

My Big, Hairy, Audacious Goal: Help 10,000 GREAT Businesses Double Revenue

In *Built to Last*, Jim Collins talks about BHAGs: Big, Hairy, Audacious Goals! As I write this book and create the systems and the team to support it, my BHAG is simple: I want to enable 10,000 already excellent businesses to double their revenue.

Why? Check out the impact. The Gartner Consulting Group describes a small business as having less than 100 employees or $50 million in revenue. Let's assume the median small business has fifty employees and $25 million in revenue and that they give 10 percent of their profits back to the community.

Based on these figures, here is what I am aiming to accomplish:

- Double the revenue of 10,000 businesses to create $250 billion in new revenue.

- Increase employment in these businesses to develop 500,000, rewarding new jobs. (This will help reemploy the "human resources" that large companies get rid of.)

- Create $12.5 billion in new annual revenue for non-profits.

- Improve communities around the world with happier families led by parents who enjoy their jobs and come home energized instead of angry.

Can this be done? I believe all of this is possible when businesses have an effective Revenue Growth Engine that is running on all cylinders. Can *you* do this? Yes! All it takes is the leadership and focus on making sure each cylinder of your Revenue Growth Engine performs at its potential.

Business is about more than making money. We can talk about the triple bottom line of return to shareholders, employees, and the community, but these returns can only happen when businesses are financially stable and growing!

This book is my gift to you. When you implement these ideas, you have the potential to multiply your revenue. This is a game-changer.

What do I ask in return?

1. Be Serious. Make building and fine-tuning your Revenue Growth Engine a core strategic priority in your company.

2. Be Open-Minded. We all have areas where we excel because we have done them for years. There may be parts of your strategy that seem small to you at first. Think of the engine in your car. If one of the cylinders stops firing on the way home today, will the others make up for it, or will you find yourself on the side of the road? The sales or marketing tactic that you are skeptical or afraid of may be the thing holding you back.

3. Be Great. We need great companies with visionary leaders. Keep doing what you do. Grow as a leader, continue inspiring operational excellence, create a great culture, and give back to your community. When you add a Revenue Growth Engine, incredible things will happen.

I hate to see great companies with visionary leaders that are not growing at the rate they could be. My goal is to change this.

Will this book get in the hands of some less-than-great companies? Probably. Without incredible leadership, dedication to the client, and employee loyalty, however, most of these large businesses will be flashes in the pan. It is the exceptional businesses that will last.

I Have Learned from Experience

Over the past quarter of a century, I have worked with hundreds of businesses. Shortly after beginning my career as a technology sales rep, I was recruited to work as a dealer sales manager for a Japanese office technology manufacturer. In this role, I spent five years working with about thirty businesses ranging from $2 million to $30 million in revenue. My goal was to support their growth with a business strategy, sales training, and marketing ideas.

During that time, I became fascinated with software. I was particularly interested in document management software, which allowed businesses to capture, organize, and secure documents scanned using their digital copiers. While the software was fascinating, what caught my attention the most was the potential for the additional offering to drive revenue growth in a rapidly maturing industry with declining profit margins.

Driven by the desire and opportunity to help these small businesses succeed, I started a sales training and marketing company. Doors opened to help companies on three continents. Over the past sixteen years, I have trained thousands of salespeople, along with rolling out initiatives for several household-name technology companies. I also became involved in digital marketing strategies and learning new skills, including website design, email, search engine optimization, social media, and, most recently, inbound marketing.

> With one foot in sales and another in marketing, I had a unique opportunity to see how all of this can work together.

With one foot in sales and another in marketing, I had a unique opportunity to see how all of this can work together. The ideas in this book are the result of seeing many successes and even more failures. They are born from the frustration of watching companies execute well in one aspect of their Revenue Growth Engine while ignoring others.

I want to end your frustration. I want you to experience results from your marketing and sales enablement efforts. If you execute one sales or marketing tactic well, but you do not see any growth, you will be able to diagnose the problems, fix your Revenue Growth Engine, and get your company back to full growth speed.

Is Your Revenue Growth Engine Generating Exponential Results?

All companies have a Revenue Growth Engine. The problem is that part of the engine runs amazingly well and gets constant attention, preventative maintenance, and repair while the rest gets neglected. When an engine is not firing on all cylinders, the vehicle will not gain the velocity it should.

As I talk with business leaders about their marketing and sales efforts, I typically see that all companies have some strategies in motion, but they are not aligned. They are also missing huge pieces of their growth engine. Instead of firing on all cylinders to move the business revenue up and to the right, they are sputtering along. Not only are the strategies not supporting each other, but they are also pulling in different directions!

The primary difference between companies that grow and companies that are stagnant is leadership involvement. Many business owners "outsource" their sales and marketing strategies to people in their company or outside companies.

Internally, this responsibility usually goes to either the sales managers or the marketing managers. Most sales managers are not familiar with current marketing or business strategies.

> As a business leader, you need to take ownership of your Revenue Growth Engine. Handing this off to others is no longer an option.

Marketing managers are generally early in their careers and hired because they are both affordable and have some "social media savvy." These people are great, but they typically do not understand the sales dynamic in business strategies. In all of this, the message of the company gets watered down at best or confused at worst.

As a business leader, you need to take ownership of your Revenue Growth Engine. Handing this off to others is no longer an option. You can hire employees and vendors to execute the strategy, but you need to oversee every aspect of it. Ownership means you need a high-level understanding of each cylinder and valve.

You need to be able to recognize when one cylinder is not firing. Then you need to lead your team to fix it. You do this in the financial and operations parts of your business. Now, it is time to do this on the revenue side. Companies can grow when they align their current sales and marketing activities toward a growth goal. When you do this, you create sustainable growth.

There are many great books about sales and marketing. The ideas presented in these books can help various aspects of your sales and marketing strategies. My intent in this book is to tie them all together. Even if you are a fan, as I am, of marketing and sales gurus like Donald Miller, Jeb Blount, Seth Godin, Brent Adamson, Matthew Dixon, Brent Adamson, and Larry Levine (my co-host of the *Selling From the Heart* podcast), you will find that this book provides a framework to tie all of your strategies together.

I am sure your business has cylinders that are going well. What you will get out of this book is a framework to see which ones perform well and which ones are not firing. If you would like to get a head start on assessing your business, download the Revenue Growth Engine Map at

www.RevenueGrowthEngine.net/free-tool-kit

While you are there, make sure to sign up to get a consistent stream of ideas that will help you fine-tune your engine.

You can also follow the Revenue Growth Engine on Twitter at **www.twitter.com/revgrowthengine**

What This Book Is Not

Growth gurus are a dime a dozen these days. Scroll through your Facebook or LinkedIn feed, and you will find sponsored ads for companies promising to grow your revenue. "Build a funnel, and they will come!" "Try my new paid advertising program, and you will have so many leads you won't know what to do."

This book is not the business equivalent of a "get rich quick" scheme. I do not offer you a silver bullet. After all, it is these one-off marketing or sales tactics that have left so many businesses disillusioned.

What I do offer you is a strategic framework you can deploy in your company through processes. This book is a serious guide to building an engine that will power your growth. Like any engine, multiple components need to work together.

Building your Revenue Growth Engine takes work. It requires leadership and vision to drive organizational change. The change is worth it.

The Promise: Revenue Growth

Whether your expansion is flat or growing, the promise is this: get your Revenue Growth Engine firing on all cylinders, and you can double your revenue. Even though it may take some time to get all the cylinders firing, that focus alone will start to move the needle.

It is possible to double your business' revenue. This is a bold statement, but in the Introduction, I will show you the simple math that will inspire you to rev your engine!

Introduction

I enjoy visiting great businesses. I love walking into an organization that is growing and staffed with enthusiastic employees that are serving happy clients. Potential employees and clients can sense positive energy. Even suppliers feel enthusiastic. When businesses grow, they have extra cash to invest in their facilities and the perks they offer to their employees. I feel inspired. Seeing it makes me happy.

At the same time, walking into an organization with stagnant growth is usually a bummer. Employees may be thankful and content, but it feels like something is off. The passion is missing. Clients are satisfied, but you certainly do not get the sense that they are raving fans. Potential employees will take a job at companies like this, but they do not seem to attract the real go-getters.

Without growth, these sleepy businesses have little to invest back into the company. Their offices are dated and even run down. Employees can barely snag a burnt cup of coffee in the break room, and the benefits are inadequate. I leave many of these businesses sad. There is no growth to fuel positive energy.

Having visited over 1,000 small and medium-sized businesses in the past twenty-two years, I have met many wonderful business owners who are good people and who have great employees selling leading products, delivering fantastic customer service, and giving back to their communities.

Why is it that some of these businesses thrive, bringing in revenue growth year after year, while others fall flat? You guessed it. The difference is the quality of the Revenue Growth Engine that drives their business.

How Does a Revenue Growth Engine Work?

An engine is a set of components organized in such a way as to create power and forward motion.

Consider an automobile. Lift the hood and you will find an engine. Unless you have an electric car, that engine has cylinders that burn gasoline (petrol for my British friends). The explosion of gas in each cylinder pushes the pistons out, driving the engine.

For an engine to be successful, the pistons need to line up in sequential order. If they are not firing in order, you have a problem. The engine certainly will not run at peak performance. It may stall or not even run at all.

The other day I was in my son-in-law's garage. In his spare time, he builds race cars. As I stood before his souped-up Mustang with the hood up, I immediately assumed the posture of most men: pretending I knew what I was talking about. (Of course, my wife came out, took one look at me, let out a little laugh, and went back inside to allow me some "man time" with my son-in-law. She knows I know way more about business than about cars.)

Even though I do not know anything about how to tune the engine of a race car, I could immediately tell that something was not right when he started the car. We stared at the noisy engine; my son-in-law explained that one of the cylinders was not firing and that this needed attention. If not, there would be no chance he could win a race.

Running an engine on only some of the cylinders damages the engine. The same is true for the Revenue Growth Engine in your business.

Here is the good news: if you can get all the cylinders firing, you can rev up the Revenue Growth Engine and experience exponential growth.

Is Doubling Your Revenue in Less Than Three Years Possible?

In the introduction to the best seller, *Atomic Habits*, James Clear tells the story of the British cycling team. By 2003, they had such a poor track record that bike companies did not want the team riding their bikes, concerned it would hurt their reputation.

Coming into this dismal situation, Dave Brailsford, the famed British cycling coach, was confident that he could make a difference. Why? He had a strategy that he referred to as "the aggregation of marginal gains." The philosophy is that if you

19

make small margins of improvement in everything that you do, you will achieve significant results.

Brailsford began breaking down bike race performance into small pieces. For example, he redesigned the bike seats, improved the tires, and even improved the bike shorts. They looked for a 1 percent improvement in all kinds of seemingly insignificant areas.

All these small improvements accumulated. The results started coming, and in less than five years, the team won 60 percent of the medals in the 2008 Olympics.

When you drive modest growth in these two key metrics, new customer growth, and selling more to existing clients, you can double revenue relatively quickly.

In our example, let's assume Company X has $5 million in revenue. They have 1,000 clients. So, their annual revenue per client is $5,000. If they want to double their business, they need to grow their client base by 12 percent and increase their average revenue per client by the same 12 percent each year.

	Today		Year 1		Year 2		Year 3
# of Clients	1000	+12%	1120	+12%	1254	+12%	1404
Rev. per Client	$5,000	+12%	$5,600	+12%	$6,272	+12%	$7,025
Total Rev.	$5.0 m		$6.3 m		$7.9 m		$9.9 m

Wow! By improving 12 percent (that is just 1 percent each month) in two key areas, you can double your business in less than three years!

What about your business? What kind of revenue growth could you see? Take a moment and do some simple math using the chart below.

	Today		Year 1		Year 2		Year 3
# of Clients		+12%		+12%		+12%	
Rev. per Client		+12%		+12%		+12%	
Total Rev.							

As a business owner, sales leader, or marketing executive, if this does not get you excited, I do not know what will! The potential for growth when you focus on bringing in more clients and growing your revenue per client is exciting!

With this excitement in mind, look back over the past three years. Have you seen this kind of growth? If so, great! The ideas in this book will help you enhance your results. If you have not seen this kind of growth, why not? What needs to change?

Why does this type of growth not happen in most businesses? The answer is simple: most companies focus on only one of the two growth drivers. They either focus on driving new clients, or they work hard on cross-selling to their existing clients. Very rarely do both drivers function well at the same time.

> Most companies focus on only one of the two growth drivers.

Think about it. If your focus was on growing net-new business, you might achieve 12 percent or more growth per year. However, if your revenue per client stays flat, in the above example, you would have grown from $5 million to $7 million. The problem is that most companies that focus on net-new business alone end up discounting to get new clients, which means that the revenue per client slides backward. As a result, 12 percent growth might only yield $6 million in revenue.

The same math works if you focus on growing revenue per client without bringing in new clients. Using the above example, if you build your revenue per client by 12 percent through adding new products and services that you can cross-sell to your client base, but neglect to bring on new clients, you will grow from $5 million to $8 million. However, in the real world, when you are not increasing your client base, you are always going to lose some to attrition. So, let's say $7 million in total to be on the safe side.

Do You Want to Grow?

Is your business great? Do you have a meaningful mission? Do you have a staff that cares? Do you sell products or services that make your clients' lives better? Do you support charitable causes in your community? If so, you have a great business!

I am a Canadian boy who fell in love with a sweet southern girl. As a result, I live in the southern United States. What I love about this country is the promise of the American Dream. It says if you work hard enough, you can have anything you want in life.

The American Dream (or for my Canadian, British, and Australian friends, and others around the world, insert whatever type of dream you want) means something different to everyone. For some, it is financial freedom for your family as you pass down a great business to your children or grandchildren. For others, it is the ability to give to the causes you care about most. Your dream may be to cash out and start your next entrepreneurial venture. Or maybe you dream about retiring and handing off the business to be owned by your employees.

Whatever your definition of the American Dream is, it needs one thing: revenue growth. Without revenue, the dream is dead.

I want you to know this: no matter where you live, the concept of the American Dream is alive, and it is doing well. All it takes is time and expertise to build and fine-tune your

23

Revenue Growth Engine. That is what I would like to coach you to do.

My Commitment to You

My commitment to you is to pour everything I have learned into this book. Over the past twenty-two years, I have seen many amazing businesses. I have talked with hundreds of visionary business owners and I have seen what works. I have also seen what does not. As an avid reader, I have benefited from the ideas of many authors.

As a salesperson, I have sat across the desk from small businesspeople, waiting quietly in the tension after asking the big closing question. I have also presented recommendations to large healthcare organizations and Fortune 500 companies.

Over the years in sales, I have had some career-changing sales wins and experienced soul-crushing losses. Having trained several thousand sales reps, I have also had a front-row seat to observe what works and what does not.

My career has also led me deep into the world of marketing. My undergraduate and MBA degrees focused on marketing. In 2004, I started a company to help medium-sized technology dealers market their businesses. We built websites and proposal templates with a focus on deploying a message that would help them win new business and cross-sell their clients into new software solutions.

Over time, our marketing practice grew to include search engine optimizations, blogging, and social media. We then took a deep dive into inbound marketing, helping companies implement strategies to move people through the awareness, consideration, and decision stages of the buying process.

Along the way, we made friends with several leading marketing automation companies. In similarity to the highs and lows in my sales career, my marketing journey has included some incredible success stories and some total bombs. In all of this, I learned about what works and what does not.

> My commitment to you is to put the best of what I have experienced in this book.

My commitment to you is to put the best of what I have experienced in this book. You will get both real-world theory and practical application born from experience. The approach is not pie-in-the-sky stuff from the halls of a university or the pages of a textbook. In each section, before I share the practical action steps, I want you to understand the "why" behind the action. When you know the "why," then the "what" will make much more sense.

Your Commitment to Your Company

I have committed to you. Now, I would like you to commit back to me.

If you have a great company, you deserve to grow. You owe it to yourself, your family, your employees, your clients, and your suppliers. They deserve to work with a vibrant organization that has financial resources.

The way you get financial resources is to grow revenue. The way you grow revenue is by building and fine-tuning your Revenue Growth Engine.

The goal of this book is: helping you grow!

What do I ask from you? Commit to act. If you do, I guarantee you will grow revenue.

The book is structured so that you can implement the four core growth strategies in one year. I do not recommend that you try to do all of them at once. Instead, after you read through the book, I will have you go back and pick one of the four areas to work on first. Spend an entire ninety days working on this part of your growth engine. Then move to the next section.

Over the year, you will have implemented and improved each core growth function. In year two, I recommend that you go back and fine-tune each of these areas throughout the four quarters. Wouldn't it be amazing if your company developed a culture going forward where you focused on a core area of your growth engine each quarter? Imagine what your company could look like in three years.

If you do all of the things I recommend in this book and you do not grow, hunt me down online, and I will send you back the money you spent on this book along with enough money to buy your lunch for your trouble. However, I think we both know that when you take affirmative action and focus on growth, you will be rewarded.

What's the Plan?

This book provides an overview of the components of a high-performance Revenue Growth Engine. Each section contains action items. Throughout the book, you will also find links to the Revenue Growth Engine website, **www.RevenueGrowthEngine.net**, where you will discover many resources to help you on your way.

In Chapter One, you will learn more about the two ways to grow revenue and the two types of experiences you need to create to make this happen. You will also see the cumulative impact of a series of small choices executed over time. To have an effective Revenue Growth Engine, you need to be crystal clear on your ideal client.

Once you are clear on whom you are selling to, we will roll up our sleeves, lift the hood, and get to work optimizing the components of your Revenue Growth Engine:

- First, we maximize the force for your engine, your ideal prospect experience, and ideal client experience.

- Next, we will improve the fuel for your engine, a focused message based on the outcomes your ideal clients desire.

- Then we will look at the four flywheels. These are like the cylinders of your engine: outbound marketing, outbound selling, client experience, and client communication. You will learn about the importance of process in each of these areas.

- Finally, we will consider the data and technology required to automate your engine.

You will leave with a game plan to improve your Revenue Growth Engine, plan budgets, and evaluate your success. You will also leave with an implementation strategy. All of this is for naught if you do not implement it.

Throughout the book, you will be building your Revenue Growth Engine plan. To help, we have put together a toolkit to help you optimize your engine: **www.RevenueGrowthEngine.net/free-tool-kit**

Are you ready to grow? Let's get growing!

Important Points

1. The #1 goal of marketing and sales is revenue growth.

2. There are only two ways to grow revenue: add net-new clients and cross-sell more to your current clients.

3. The two core measurements for marketing and sales are:

    a. Net-New: Total Number of Clients

    b. Cross-Sell: Revenue Per Client

4. Your Revenue Growth Engine is the total of your marketing and sales processes.

Darrell Amy

Chapter 1: Building Your Revenue Growth Engine

Imagine where you would be if you doubled your business every three years? Ten years from now, you would have a business that doubled three times! If your business is doing $10 million in revenue now, it could be at $80 million in a short space of time. Think about what you could do with the increased income. See the jobs you could create. Visualize the impact you would have on your community and the world. Of course, I do not have to encourage you to think about how this would be a game-changer for you and your family.

Is this kind of growth possible? Yes! You just need to ensure your Revenue Growth Engine is running on all cylinders.

What Is an Engine?

Merriam-Webster defines the word engine as follows: "A machine for converting any of various forms of energy into mechanical force and motion." The engine in your car converts gasoline or electricity into a force that moves your vehicle forward.

Your company's Revenue Growth Engine converts marketing and sales energy into increased clients and purchases, which cause your revenue to grow.

Some engines perform better than others. A lawnmower has a motor; so does a BMW. The lawnmower engine has two cylinders. Even if those two cylinders are operating at peak performance, there is only so much that the engine can do.

A BMW 760i has twelve cylinders. When those cylinders operate at peak performance, the car has 601 horsepower. This "ultimate driving machine" will get you places fast.

Not Running on All Cylinders

Lift the hood on most businesses, and you will discover a Revenue Growth Engine with only a handful of cylinders running.

Let's say you took your BMW 760i and unplugged half of the spark plugs so that only six of the twelve cylinders were firing. How would the car run? I am no mechanic, but I am guessing the car would not run well if it ran at all.

Imagine taking that car to the BMW dealership and complaining that you were not getting the horsepower promised on the brochure. How crazy would that be?

Lift the hood on most businesses, and you will discover a Revenue Growth Engine with only a handful of cylinders running. The management team invests heavily in one or two cylinders and then feels frustrated that the growth engine is delivering less than optimal results.

As the CEO of a digital marketing agency, I saw this repeatedly. We would find a sales-focused company that was running a great outbound prospecting cylinder. They would drive their reps to prospect, but never took the time to segment their market and identify target accounts.

In the rush of prospecting, they also neglected to optimize their sales tools. Every rep used different presentations and proposals, and most of them were outdated. As a result, the prospecting funnel was never as efficient as it could be. This led to rep frustration and burnout.

There was one company we worked with that focused on growing net-new business. They wanted some leads, so they hired us to get them on Google. We told them that they needed to consider what happened once someone found their website. How would they convert those visitors to leads?

Then, how would those leads get qualified and handed off to sales? It was like they wanted to invest in improving one cylinder, but ignored the other two cylinders related to it.

After a month of working with us, this company ended up being frustrated with the results of the sales team and angry with the marketing team. They were only running two of the six cylinders for net-new business revenue growth.

They had recently invested in a new program to cross-sell to their clients. The intention was that their current clients would buy into this new service, and it would help offset the declining profit margins in their existing products, which were quickly becoming commoditized.

Every Monday, the sales manager would badger the sales team to talk to their current clients about this new service. However, the company did not have a periodic business review system in place. Reps had no plan to meet with existing clients until they were ready for renewal.

On top of that, the company had no clear onboarding process or ongoing communication strategy to let their clients know about the new services the company offered.

If you surveyed the current client base, my guess is most of them did not even know their vendor offered these additional services. No wonder they could not get the results they wanted!

Here is the point. If you want an engine to grow your business, you need multiple cylinders. These cylinders need to be firing at peak performance.

What Are the Components of a Revenue Growth Engine?

Each part of the engine has an important function, so does a revenue growth engine. Here is a high-level overview of the components.

Sources of Revenue

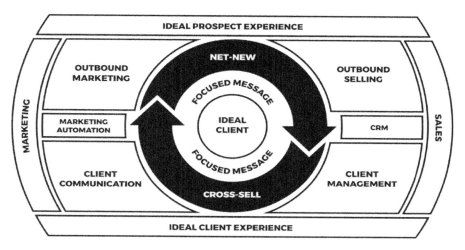

As discussed in the Introduction, there are only two sources of revenue: net-new business and cross-selling more to existing clients. Design your revenue growth engine to drive both net-new and cross-sell. When you do this, you begin to realize exponential revenue growth.

Goal: More Ideal Clients

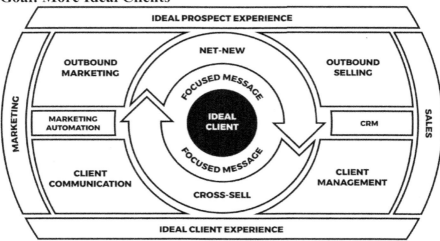

Ideal Clients are at the center of your Revenue Growth Engine. These are the type of clients that can buy everything you offer. They are an excellent fit for your company. You enjoy working with them because they value what you do and give you referrals. They even pay their bills on time.

These are the type of clients that will grow your business. In the following chapters, you will take a deep dive into the profile of your ideal client. You will also determine the financial impact they can have on your revenue. Most companies discover that their ideal clients generate 10X, 20X, or more revenue than an average client. Sure, you will take some average clients, but to grow, you need to land and retain ideal clients. This is the heart of the engine.

Force: Ideal Prospect and Client Experience

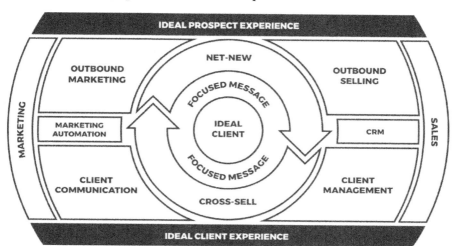

A powerful engine has force. With enough force, you can accelerate quickly and pull a big load. The energy for your Revenue Growth Engine comes from your Ideal Prospect and Client Experiences.

When you go to a Disney theme park, you can tell that they have put a lot of thought into the experience. From the time you get out of your car and go through the park entrance to the enjoyment of each ride, everything centers on making the experience amazing. As a result, millions of people stream into their parks each year.

You may not be a theme park, but your prospects and clients have experience with your company. The less friction and the more memorable your experience, the more trust and confidence you build. These are the levers that move your business forward faster. In the Ideal Client Experience chapter, you will learn how to map and optimize your client experience.

Fuel: A Focused Message

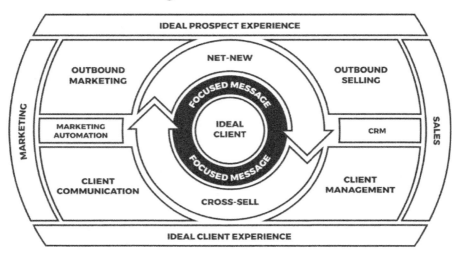

Every engine needs the right kind of fuel. The fuel for your Revenue Growth Engine is a focused message. Like all of us, your ideal prospects and clients are exposed to thousands of messages and advertisements every day. We all have finely tuned filters. Only things that are important to us get through.

What is essential to your ideal clients? They are on high alert for ideas that will help them get the outcomes they want, which includes achieving their goals and solving their problems.

I firmly believe that buyers do not buy your products and services; they buy the outcomes your products and services create.

In the Focused Message section of the book, you will learn how to understand the outcomes your ideal prospects and clients want.

You will also learn how to create an outcomes inventory, a catalog of all the results you can deliver. The inventory will become the ingredients for all of your marketing and sales messages.

Flywheels: Sales and Marketing Processes

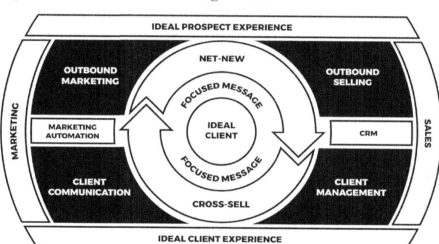

An engine needs to sustain motion. Think of the power of a spinning flywheel. The flywheels in your engine are the marketing and sales processes that support net-new business and cross-selling.

Boil any business down to its most basic level, and you find two things: people and procedures. Processes make things repeatable. Methods can also be optimized. As Gino Wickman says in the book, Traction, "Nothing can be fine-tuned until it's first consistent."

The challenge is that many marketing and sales teams do not have documented processes. In this book, you will discover four key process areas. These are like the cylinders of your Revenue Growth Engine.

Net-New	Cross-Sell
1. Outbound Marketing	3. Client Management
2. Outbound Sales	4. Client Communication

Two of the Revenue Growth Engine cylinders are related to driving net-new business: outbound marketing and outbound sales. The other two are related to cross-selling more to your clients: client management and client communication.

Get Net-New Clients

New clients are the lifeblood of every business. A properly-tuned Revenue Growth Engine ensures you are on the radar of ideal prospects with outbound marketing and sales processes. The goal is 100 percent coverage meaning that every key decision-maker or influencer in your ideal prospects hears from your company regularly with valuable insights on how they can achieve their outcomes.

Outbound Marketing

Traditional marketing focuses on getting leads. You do not need leads if you already know who your ideal prospects are.

Instead, you need engagement with these prospects. You need to be on their radar.

Outbound marketing processes combine multiple channels of communication, sharing helpful insights related to the outcomes they desire. It begins with a process to send relevant messages on multiple channels, including email, direct mail, social media, and targeted advertising.

These messages are highly targeted either to individual accounts or specific buyer personas. Next, you need processes to listen and engage, tailoring the message, and responding based on signals and triggers from your ideal prospects. All of this works together to ensure you have 100 percent coverage of your ideal prospects.

Outbound Selling

While the goal of outbound marketing is to provide coverage to get on the radar of ideal prospects, the purpose of outbound selling is to build relationships in these accounts. It begins with a target account process that ensures every ideal prospect is assigned to a salesperson. The process includes the expected cadence for outreach.

Next, you need a prospecting strategy. Salesforce.com research showed that it takes 6–8 touches with a prospect to get an appointment.[i] This takes a process. Another process you need relates to engaging the entire buying team during a sales cycle. With today's world of B2B buying teams, you need tools and tactics to reach each person that influences the buying decision.

Cross-Sell Current Clients

The second half of the Revenue Growth Engine drives cross-selling. The goal is to sell more products, services, or solutions to your existing clients so that you can increase your average revenue per client. The challenge is that many companies do a poor job of letting clients know about additional products from which they could benefit.

There are two parts to the cross-selling motion. The first client management has to do with sales. The second client communication is related to marketing. Together, these create your client experience.

Client Management

The way your sales team manages your client relationships determines how well you cross-sell. The first stage of client management is onboarding. Not only should the onboarding experience be memorable, but it should also set the stage for additional sales.

Next are periodic business reviews. Depending on the size and potential of the client, you should meet with them on a regular schedule to review your performance, suggest improvements, and showcase additional products, services, and solutions you could bring to the table. The third component of a client management strategy is your renewal process.

Client Communication

How often do your clients hear from you? Ironically, most companies use email to spam non-clients while they neglect to communicate with the clients who have permitted them to communicate.

Your clients should hear from you regularly. When they do, communication should always include additional ways you could help.

An effective communication strategy includes regular communication cadence, like a client newsletter. The second component is the cross-selling messages. These are messages targeted at segments of your client base that are a great fit for specific products, services, or solutions. The third component of a cross-sell strategy is client events where you invite targeted groups of clients to experience additional ways your company could help them.

Data and Technology

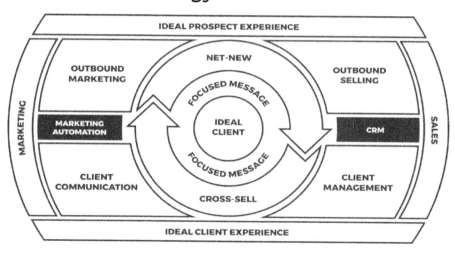

Just as all of today's vehicles use data and technology to optimize the performance of the engine, your Revenue Growth Engine also requires data and technology.

Most companies are frustrated about the quality of their prospect and client data. I have discovered that while it may feel impossible to maintain data for every single client and prospect, when you narrow it down to maintaining accurate data for ideal prospects and clients, the task becomes much more manageable. Keeping your data current is not a one-time event. In the chapter on data, you will learn how to build a process to ensure your data stays current.

You need marketing and sales technology. It needs to work together, seamlessly sharing data. When we look at what we call the revenue technology (revtech) stack in a company, we typically find one of two things: they either have way too many platforms, or there is hardly anything at all. Given that there are well over a thousand vendors in the marketing automation and sales enablement spaces, it is no wonder there is confusion and paralysis when it comes to technology. If you want to find out more about technology in your business go to www.RevenueGrowthEngine.net/technology

Rating Your Revenue Growth Engine

Before we go further, let's pause for a moment and take an inventory. How is your Revenue Growth Engine doing?

Based on what you have learned, rate the effectiveness of each component of your Revenue Growth Engine on a scale of 1–10.

	Excellent									**Poor**
Prospect Experience	1	2	3	4	5	6	7	8	9	10
Client Experience	1	2	3	4	5	6	7	8	9	10
A Focused Message	1	2	3	4	5	6	7	8	9	10
Outbound Marketing	1	2	3	4	5	6	7	8	9	10
Outbound Sales	1	2	3	4	5	6	7	8	9	10
Client Management	1	2	3	4	5	6	7	8	9	10
Client Communication	1	2	3	4	5	6	7	8	9	10
Technology and Data	1	2	3	4	5	6	7	8	9	10

The area where you gave yourself the lowest score is the place where you could probably see the quickest returns. The lowest-scoring component is the low-hanging fruit for the growth of your organization. Get this area right, and you have a good shot at moving towards the growth that could double your revenue.

What Now?

Over the coming chapters, we will take a close look at each cylinder in your Revenue Growth Engine. As you proceed through each chapter, I encourage you to take notes on the specific areas that you could improve. The goal is to build a strategic plan to fine-tune your growth engine.

To help with this, I put together the Revenue Growth Engine Tool Kit. On this page, you will find the Revenue Growth

Engine checkup along with many other resources that will help you on your journey. You can find this on our website at **www.RevenueGrowthEngine.net/free-tool-kit.**

Are you ready to grow? Let's get to work!

Important Points

1. Most businesses' Revenue Growth Engine only has a handful of cylinders running.

2. The fuel for your Revenue Growth Engine is a focused message. If your message is clear and resonates with your buyers, then you have good fuel.

3. The force for your Revenue Growth Engine is your Ideal Prospect Experience and Ideal Client Experience.

4. You need marketing and sales processes that drive net-new and cross-sell business.

5. Two of the Revenue Growth Engine processes are related to net-new business: outbound marketing and outbound selling.

6. Two of the Revenue Growth Engine components support cross-selling: client management (sales) and client communication (marketing).

7. You need processes to maintain data on your ideal prospects and clients.

8. You need the right mix of marketing and sales technology (revtech) to support your engine.

Darrell Amy

Section 1: The Force - Ideal Client Experience

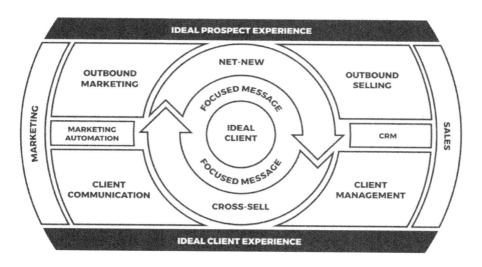

or an engine to accelerate quickly, it needs torque, the force that propels the vehicle forward. The force for your Revenue Growth Engine is your ideal client experience. These are the clients that can move your business forward faster. They can buy everything that you sell. They also value what you do, they trust your advice, and they give referrals.

In this section, you will identify your ideal client. You will learn how to evaluate the impact of these ideal clients on your revenue. Then you will discover strategies to enhance the ideal prospect experience and ideal client experience.

Chapter 2: Define Your Ideal Client

A ll clients are not equal. Your ideal clients are more valuable than other clients.

Vilfredo Pareto was a European economist famous for the 80/20 rule. In the late 1800s, he noticed that 20 percent of the people in Italy owned about 80 percent of the land. This pattern began to show up in many different areas—especially business.

Sort your list of clients by annual revenue. Add up the revenue from the top 20 percent of your clients. If you have 1,000 clients, add up the revenue from your top 200 clients. If Pareto is correct (and he almost always is), you will discover that these ideal clients are the ones driving your business.

What would it mean if you could get more of these ideal clients?

Recently, I was leading a company through a Revenue Growth Workshop. After discussing their growth goals, we began to talk about their favorite clients. Going around the conference table, each of the key leaders shared a specific client that they loved. For each client, I asked what they liked about the relationship.

As we wrote the names of these clients on the whiteboard along with their characteristics, several trends began emerging. These clients valued the relationship they had with the company, saw them as more than just a vendor, and were open to new ideas. These clients were slightly bigger than the average customer. Because of their size, they had some unique challenges, which the company could meet. These clients also had the potential to purchase additional products and services from the company.

Next, I asked about their average "bread and butter" clients. In stark contrast to the ideal client, most of these clients did not value the relationship. It was not uncommon for them to solicit proposals from other vendors at each contract renewal. While most of them renewed, they used competitive quotes to erode profitability. Others left for competitors. Either way, the sales team worked hard to get lower and lower profits. After the sale, many of them were demanding. Some were outright unreasonable, causing frustration in the service department.

Next, I asked the team what the average purchase amount was from their average client. In this case, the purchase was $7,500, followed by $2,500 in revenue for a service contract. Over ten years, if the client renewed their contract three times, the company could expect $30,000 in revenue. (However, many of these transactional companies changed vendors to get a better deal, so the real number was lower than $30,000.)

In contrast, I asked about the revenue from ideal clients. The sale averaged $75,000, with $25,000 in trailing revenue. Over ten years, the company expected about $300,000 from this client. Trust and value are the foundation of these relationships, so the renewal rate was much higher.

Pareto's 80/20 rule was in full effect. The majority of the revenue was coming from a handful of ideal clients.

> Not only were these clients more enjoyable to serve but landing just one of them was equivalent to landing at least ten average clients.

At this point, I trust you are having the same "a-ha" moment that this management team had. The company's ideal clients were worth ten times an average client. Not only were these clients more enjoyable to serve but landing just one of them was equivalent to landing at least ten average clients.

However, it gets better. Most of the ideal clients had additional needs beyond the core product. This particular company had a new set of services that were an excellent fit for these mid-sized companies. The average annual revenue from these new services is $30,000 a year per client. Over ten years, that meant an additional $300,000 in potential revenue!

With the potential to cross-sell additional services, these ideal clients were worth an average of $600,000 over ten years! That is twenty times the value of an average client.

Now the team was fired up. If the business could attract more ideal clients, they could hit their aggressive growth goals.

Darrell Amy

While the team agreed that they would still sell to average clients, the consensus was that they wanted to focus their sales and marketing efforts around the ideal client.

In his fascinating book, *The Pumpkin Plan*, Mike Michalowicz uses the analogy of a prize-winning pumpkin farmer. Farmers that want to grow big pumpkins focus their energy on the big pumpkins. When you do this, you create an environment in which your pumpkins can thrive. You get more ideal clients.

> A client sees you as a transactional vendor that sells them a product or service. A client sees you as a trusted partner.

Average businesses end up focusing most of their energy on the 80 percent "bread and butter" clients. They reason that these are the ones who pay the bills. While that may be true right now, the key to the future of your business is to identify the characteristics of your ideal client and attract more clients that match their profile.

Who are your favorite clients? What would it mean to your business if the majority of your clients looked like them?

Clients vs. Customers

In this book, I talk about clients instead of customers. I believe there is a big difference between a customer and a client. A customer sees you as a transactional vendor that sells them a product or service. A client sees you as a trusted partner.

On the loyalty scale, customers tend toward low loyalty, willing to switch vendors for a lower price. Clients recognize the value of not only your product or service but also the other ways you add value. You are integrated into their business; thus, they tend to be much more loyal.

All clients are not equal. Some clients are more valuable than others. They not only bring more revenue and profit; they also appreciate you. Building your business to serve these clients is smart. When you do this, you improve your chances of retaining them. You also set yourself up to attract more of them. To add, cross-sell, and retain ideal clients, you need to identify your perfect prospect and then build an exceptional client experience. Let's explore each of these.

Define Your Ideal Client

The first step is to define your ideal client. Ask yourself, "What do my favorite clients have in common?"

Look at your current client base. Sit down with some of your sales leaders and identify a handful of your favorite clients. Your wish is for every client to be an ideal client. Consider the following questions:

1. What do we like about working with this company?

- Do we work with them easily?

- Do they have a significant and ongoing need for our products?

- Do they pay their bills on time?

- Do they look to you for multiple products and services?

- How much money have we made from these clients?

2. What do the clients like about working with us?

- How do they benefit from our products and services?

- Do they value our advice?

- What do they appreciate about our customer service?

3. What are their demographics?

- How many employees do they have?

- What is their industry?

- Do they have specific traits that make them a good candidate, such as using certain ERP software?

- What types of people (for example, CEO, CFO, HR manager) do we typically work with in these companies?

Creating a profile of your ideal client focuses your outbound efforts on prospecting to the accounts that will build a solid future for your reps and your company.

Obviously, you want more of these ideal clients. Later in the book, in the outbound selling chapter, I will address how to create a target account program that identifies these ideal prospects, assigns them to a sales rep, and ensures they hear from your company. I will also show how you can create a client loyalty program to ensure the retention of these ideal clients.

Right now, I want you to identify your ideal client. Print these questions and put them on your desk. Go ahead and make some copies and put them on everyone's desk.

Determine the Impact of an Ideal Client

Once you identify your ideal client, you need to determine the impact they have on your revenue.

To do this, I recommend that you add up everything this client could buy from you over the next ten years. This list will show how an ideal client could impact your revenue if you optimize your engine to cross-sell all of your products and services.

While you are looking at the impact of your ideal client, I recommend you also look at the ten-year impact of an average client. Similar to the illustration above, add up what they could purchase over ten years. When you put an average client with an ideal client, you see a stark contrast.

The point here is simple: ideal clients drive growth.

You may be thinking, "What about my average clients—we don't want to ignore them." True. I am not saying you stop taking care of your average clients. But from a business growth standpoint, you need to 100 percent, absolutely, without fail, make sure that you are intentionally building your Revenue Growth Engine to attract and maximize the value from ideal clients.

If you are still concerned, consider this: most of your average clients aspire to become like your ideal clients. As you focus your message on the outcomes your ideal clients want, your average clients will tune in as well.

In the next chapter, we turn our attention to how to create an amazing experience for your ideal prospects and clients.

Important Points

1. All clients are not equal. Your ideal clients are more valuable than other clients.

2. Landing an ideal client is equivalent to landing at least ten average clients.

3. A customer sees you as a transactional vendor that sells them a product or service. A client sees you as a trusted partner.

4. The first step is to define your ideal client. Ask yourself, "What do my favorite clients have in common?"

5. Once you identify your ideal client, you need to determine the impact they have on your revenue compared to an average client.

Darrell Amy

Chapter 3: Create Your Ideal Client Experience

O nce you have identified your ideal clients, you need to obsess over them. What do they want? How can you serve them better?

In 1998, Joseph Pine and James Gilmore prophetically declared in their *Harvard Business Review* article, "Welcome to the experience economy."[ii] In the early part of the last century, the agrarian economy changed to a product economy. In the latter part of the century, we transitioned to a services economy. Now, we live in an experience economy.

Let's be honest; there probably is not a whole lot of difference between your products and those of your competitors. Even though you think you provide the best service in town, the reality is that most of your competitors provide great service as well.

How do you differentiate yourself? You do this through the experience you provide to your buyers and clients—this is what sets you apart. In the context of revenue growth, you want to obsessively consider the experience your ideal clients desire.

There are two phases to the client experience: buyer experience and client experience. At each stage of this experience, you need to put yourself in their shoes and consider two things:

- What are they thinking?

- What questions do they have?

Let's explore these questions for both the buyer and client.

Think about a recent purchase you have made. What steps did you go through?

Every buyer goes through a journey when they make a purchase: awareness, consideration, and decision.[iii]

Awareness: I am aware I have a problem, but I need to define it. At this point, today's buyer hits the search engines and begins asking their group of trusted advisors.

Consideration: I am considering options to solve the problem.

Decision: I am ready to take action.

These steps happen for individual buyers as well as for business buying teams.

What might your ideal prospect be thinking at each stage of their journey? What questions might they have?

Let's pretend we are an HR manager of an ideal prospect. In our fictional scenario, some new laws require companies to have their workers review and re-sign their employment agreements and employee handbooks annually.

Like any buyer, there are outcomes, concerns, and questions at each stage.

Awareness:

- **Thoughts**: I want to be successful in my job. I want to make sure our company is compliant and does not get penalized.

- **Questions**: Do these laws apply to us? If so, how do we need to respond? What are the penalties for not complying?

Consideration: Now that I know we are going to have to make some changes to comply with these new laws, I need to figure out what the options are.

- **Thoughts**: I want to do the right thing for our company. I think about how other companies are tackling this problem.

- **Questions**: What are the best options? How are other companies doing this? How much would that cost? How much time would this involve on our part? Who would need to be involved? Can we do this with our internal processes, or is there a better way to get this done? What would have the least impact on our organization?

Decision: I think we need to outsource this.

WHAT ARE OUR 7 TOUCHES

63

- **Thoughts:** I want to make a good decision about this. We have got a lot going on now, but I know this needs to get done.

- **Questions:** Who is the best partner to manage this for us? Are there guarantees? What is the process of engaging them? How long will it take to get done?

As you can see, the buyer has many questions in the process of acquiring your product or service. To create a great buyer experience, does it not make sense to anticipate and answer their questions?

Smart companies do not leave the buyer experience to chance. Instead, they write the story and envision how they would like their prospects to experience the company. Let's continue our previous scenario about new employment laws.

1. Awareness: Sue, the HR manager for ABC Company, an ideal client with 200 employees headquartered in our area, reads about the new employment laws in the newsletter she gets from the state employee association. It reminds her of a voicemail she got last week from one of our company sales reps offering to come to talk with her about the challenge faced by the new laws.

Wondering if this is a problem for other similar companies, she emails three of her HR colleagues who work elsewhere. They are concerned as well. One of them forwards an email that they received from one of your sales reps that includes a link to a blog article on your website explaining how the rules may impact local companies.

Next, Sue hits Google to find out more about the extent of the problem and the penalties. One of the top search results links to a blog article on your website. She bookmarks it to read later. Later that day, as she is checking her LinkedIn feed, she sees the article again. It has been shared by one of your sales reps.

Clicking on the article, she begins to read. Further down the article, she sees a link to a special report, "Five Steps to Comply with New Employment Regulations." It looks interesting, so she downloads it, and prints a copy to read later.

At that moment, your lead manager receives a notification that Sue has downloaded the special report. Checking into the marketing automation system, he is able to see that Sue had read the blog article and visited a few other pages on the site. He sends out an email offering to provide additional assistance, but does not hear back.

2. Consideration: Sue brings up the issue at the weekly executive meeting. The CFO already has this on his radar, as he received a call and an email on the topic from your rep. The CEO also saw one of your specialists speak on the issue at her Rotary Club meeting.

The team agrees that it is time to consider different options. Sue reaches into her bag and pulls out a copy of your company's special report. Then, she forwards the email with the report to the rest of the management team.

Back at the office, your lead manager is notified that several different people from the company are coming to your website. He packages up the intel and forwards it on to the field sales rep to follow up.

Before making the call, your field sales rep reviews Sue's LinkedIn profile and Twitter feed. He learns that she is a chairperson for the state HR, along with one of your current clients. He sends an email to Sue, thanking her for downloading the report. He attaches a copy of a case study where you helped another local company solve the problem.

Sue is open to meeting with your sales rep. The following day, they have a good conversation about the special report and how other companies are solving the problem. He is able to answer several of her questions about the rough price range and how much time it will take to solve the problem.

After meeting with Sue, he sends her a thank you note. Knowing that the CFO, CEO, and IT manager are usually involved, he looks them up on LinkedIn. He sends a connection request, along with a link to a blog article about the importance of solving this problem.

3. Decision: Now it was time to figure out how to solve the problem. After reading the special report, rather than trying to do it internally, Sue believed it was smarter to hire someone else to do the work.

Over the past week, Sue reached out to a few other companies. Several were out-of-state and did not have local reps. The phone reps called. One local company sent a sales rep over to knock on her door thirty minutes after she went to their website to request information. He seemed laser-focused on selling something, but he did not ask about her needs.

Meanwhile, Sue received a detailed recommendation from your company. It not only outlined the price, but also gave a detailed implementation plan. Attached to the proposal was another case study, along with six references. Sue forwarded these documents to the rest of the executive team.

Sue invited the sales rep to present the recommendation to the executive team on their weekly Skype meeting. Before the meeting, the sales rep forwarded an email with a video of several key leaders answering common questions that most buyers have.

He presented the recommendations in a short, professional PowerPoint that included references and ended in an implementation plan. The executive team agreed it was a good idea and approved the order.

Sue, along with the rest of the executive team, felt great about the decision. They wished that all their problems were that easy to solve.

Now, that is a good story! What would it look like if you gave that amount of attention to detail in crafting the experience you would like for your ideal buyers?

Will every client story be the same? No. However, if you can envision what you would like your ideal buyer experience to look like, you can build your Revenue Growth Engine with processes and messages to deliver this experience.

Client Experience

Once you land a client, what happens? From the time they say "yes," throughout the lifetime of the relationship, the experience your clients have with your company will determine the total revenue you get from their account. Provide a poor experience, and it could be "one and done," as they move on to a competitor that promises something better. Craft a great experience, and you improve your client retention while protecting your ideal clients from competitors. You also set the stage for cross-selling additional products or services, increasing your overall revenue for the account.

> Client experience may be the best place to grow a competitive advantage. This is where you create raving fans.

Client experience may be the best place to grow a competitive advantage. This is where you create raving fans.

I learned the value of client experience from my wife. As a photographer of newborns, she captures the joy of the first days of a baby's life. What she produces is more than photographs. She creates heirloom art that her clients proudly display and cherish.

On their own, the pictures speak for themselves. However, I have watched my wife layer an amazing client experience on top of her artistry. The genius is in creating a relaxing and memorable experience for the mom.

She begins setting up the experience during the booking process. By the time the family arrives for the appointment, they are excited. The atmosphere of her studio has been thought through to the smallest detail. When the photos are ready, she could simply email them. Instead, she invites the family back for a gallery premiere that begins with a custom video of their newborn. When the photos are ready to deliver, she packages them in such a way that you can tell she cares about her business.

The experience is impressive. My wife has seen a reasonable conversion rate in cross-selling the first-year photo package. She also has fantastic client retention and gets many referrals.

Your client experience creates a competitive advantage. Fortunately for you, most of your competitors have not considered their client experience. As a result, they miss out on opportunities to cross-sell additional products and services. They also do not get the valuable referrals that they could be receiving.

To craft an ideal client experience, consider the stages of becoming a client:

1. **Onboarding**: I just spent a lot of money. I also took the risk of changing how we do things. I wonder if I made a good decision.
2. **Management:** I need to know if the product or service is performing. Am I getting my expected return on investment?
3. **Renewal**: Depending on what you sell, it is time to renew or upgrade. Do I want to continue working with

this company? How easy (or hard) will it be to maintain the relationship?

Much like the buyer experience, each step of the client experience includes moments that could hurt or enhance the relationship. As Warren Buffet says, it takes twenty years to build a reputation and only a moment to destroy it. Similarly, it takes a lot of work to win a net-new client, and a poor client experience can destroy it.

What do your ideal clients want? Similar to the buyer experience, as you craft your client experience, think about these two things:

1. What are they thinking?
2. What questions do they have?

Just as wise companies do not leave the buyer experience to chance, smart companies design their ideal client experience. Let's continue our previous scenario about new employment laws.

1. Onboarding: Sue and the executive team approved the deal. The sales rep sent her digital documents to sign, making the contracting process simple. As soon as the paperwork was received, the rep immediately sent back an email thanking her for the order and clearly explaining the process for onboarding.

The sales rep then put together a thank you card for Sue, along with a box of chocolates. At the same time, an email was sent to the owner's administrative assistant reminding him to prepare a thank you letter from the owner to the CEO of the new client welcoming them onboard.

Before the user training, the rep sent Sue a welcome letter and agenda for all of the attendees. When the attendees arrived at the training, they found a branded coffee cup, pen, and a "getting started" guide at their desks. At the end of the training, they all received a personalized certificate.

Two weeks after the training, the sales rep stopped by the office with a dozen fresh donuts with the company sticker on top. They walked through the office to answer questions.

One month later, the rep met with Sue to ensure that all the details of the rollout had gone smoothly. During this meeting, the rep explained the quarterly business review process and scheduled the first quarterly meeting.

2. Management: At the first quarterly business review, the sales rep used a branded PowerPoint presentation that included the company's business goals, the progress, and the results. Next, he introduced the Platinum Pro program, a client loyalty program developed with a set of perks needed for the ideal client. Sue was delighted with the additional benefits.

One of the benefits of the program was a free annual HR security audit. Given the sensitive information in her department, Sue welcomed the third-party review. The rep emailed a copy of a special report, "Five Key Security Risks

HR Departments Face." Sue sent this to her team, along with a note letting them know about the audit.

In the next quarterly business review, the team presented Sue with the results of the security audit in a professional binder. This began a new sales cycle for the company's security offering. The rep also asked Sue for a reference to another ideal prospect that he wanted to meet. Sue was happy to help.

One year into the program, Sue enthusiastically agreed to be featured on a video case study. She also spoke at the company's annual open house, sharing how much she loved working with this company.

3. Renewal: Fast forward two years. Sue had implemented three of the company's offerings. The finance department was also using the company's products. However, the contract was up for renewal.

The rep started sending Sue a series of emails, letting her know about the benefits of the latest version of the company's product. In the next quarterly business review, they discussed the benefits of upgrading to the next level of service.

Instead of making the renewal a chore, the company threw a thank-you party for Sue's team, catering in lunch, and highlighting all of the benefits of the new product they would be receiving. After lunch, Sue approved the new agreement, as she was happy with the value of the relationship.

What is your ideal client experience? How do you anticipate needs and answer questions along the way? What does that mean to your company?

As you can see, the more that your potential buyers and clients get touchpoints from you, the more likely they are to hire you and then continue to renew year after year.

What is the overall experience that your prospects and clients have when dealing with you? Be honest. If you read this chapter and you are feeling a twinge of guilt, then it is time to review your processes and introduce new ones.

If this is something that you need help with, book a free consultation with one of my Certified Revenue Growth Engine Implementers at **www.RevenueGrowthEngine.net/get-started.** We work with companies big and small to design and implement plans that bring the complete buying experience to life!

Important Points

1. Once you have identified your ideal clients, you need to obsess over them. What do they want? How can you serve them better?

2. There are two phases to the client experience: buyer experience and client experience.

3. Every buyer goes through a journey when they make a purchase: awareness, consideration, and decision.

4. Once you land a client, what happens? From the time they say "yes," throughout the lifetime of the relationship, the experience your clients have with your company will determine the total revenue you get from their account.

Section 2: The Fuel – A Focused Message

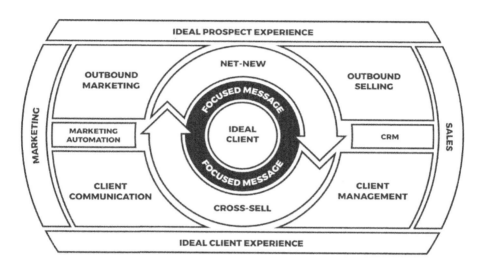

The fuel for your Revenue Growth Engine is a message that focuses on the outcomes your ideal prospects and clients want. This message needs to be consistent across marketing and sales. In this section, you will learn how to focus your message on business outcomes. Then you will learn how to deploy that consistent message across your marketing and sales.

Darrell Amy

Chapter 4: Focus Your Message on Outcomes

One of the biggest benefits of having grown up in Canada is maple syrup. There is nothing like it, especially when you helped to make it. It is probably the reason I love it so much. I remember those early spring Saturday mornings at the sugar farm when we would head out into a grove of maple trees.

Each tree had a spigot with a small bucket attached. Sweet sap would drip into the bucket, and then we would gather those buckets of sap and bring them to the sugar shack. That was where the magic happened.

A boiler sat in the middle of the shack. On top of a firebox was a large cauldron of maple sap where it would boil down into thick, delicious maple syrup within a few hours. I will never forget sitting on a log in the middle of the woods eating hot pancakes drenched in that fresh sweetness.

When it's straight out of the tree, maple sap tastes like water with a few granules of sugar. When it is boiled down, the syrup emerges. It takes about forty gallons of maple sap to make one gallon of maple syrup. It is no wonder that it is so valuable and tastes so good.

Imagine if you took the same approach to your company's message. Most companies have watered-down messages. Much like the maple sap, the ingredients are there. They just need to be boiled down to something sweet and attractive.

What Business Are You In?

Theodore Levitt, the Harvard Business School professor and father of modern marketing, understood the importance of a clear message. He challenges all of us with this question: What business are you in?[iv]

When you get this answer right, everything comes into focus. When you get this answer wrong, you not only have a hard time articulating your value proposition, you also face a highly uncertain future.

When Levitt first wrote these words in the 1950s, railroads were starting to feel the pressure from the growing trucking and airline industries. Ask any good railroad employee what they did, and they would proudly say, "We're in the railroad business." However, if you asked any customer of the railroads what the railroads did for them, they would answer differently. A businessperson would probably say that the railroads got their products from the factory to the customer. An individual traveler would say that the railroad took them where they wanted to go faster than driving.

> The railroads were not in the railroad business. They were in the *transportation* business.

The railroads were not in the railroad business. They were in the *transportation* business. Had they realized this, they would have listened to their clients and diversified into transport trucks and airplanes. Their message to their clients could have been clear and compelling: "We deliver things to people quickly and on schedule." Instead, their message was, "We drive trains. Need a train?"

What do you do? If Theodore Levitt sat in your office today and asked the question, "What business are you in?" how would you answer?

The way to get to the correct answer is to focus on your buyer. Specifically, you need to think about the outcomes they desire.

Buyers Do Not Buy Products, They Buy Outcomes

What you sell and what your clients want are two different things. We think we sell products and services. What our clients buy are outcomes.

Levitt put it brilliantly: "People do not buy drill bits, they buy holes." Your prospects do not want to buy drill bits or electric drills. They need holes. They do not want to buy your product; they need the outcomes your products or services deliver.

For example, business owners do not buy color printers; they buy color printouts. If you boil that down even further, they do not really buy color prints. If they are printing invoices, what they are buying is the ability to collect money faster from their clients. If they are printing marketing material, what they are buying is a competitive advantage and business growth.

One company can send out sales reps to sell color printers to people that do not want one or have the budget allocated. The next company, realizing that people buy outcomes, can send their sales team out to help prospects streamline their collection process or grow their revenue. How do you achieve these outcomes? With color printers, of course!

By selling products, the first company will only get the attention of the small percentage of those who are "in the market" for a color printer. By selling outcomes, the second company will be able to get the attention of the large percentage of the market that wants a streamlined collection process or to grow their business.

To fuel your revenue growth engine, you need to present a clear message that resonates with your prospects and clients. How do you do this? Focus on outcomes!

Start Your Message with "Why"

Simon Sinek captured the business world's attention when he delivered his famous TED Talk, "Start with Why."[v] This sparked a revolution of people realizing that it is not "what you do" or "how you do it" that captures people's attention. Rather, it is "why they should care" that matters.

In our pursuit of a clear message to your clients, think about it this way:

Product = What You Do

Service = How You Do It

Why Any Buyer Cares = The Outcomes You Deliver

Every day, you answer the question over and over again to your prospects and clients: "Why should I give you a shred of my attention in the middle of a hyper-busy, over-messaged day?" Your answer should be clear: "We deliver the outcomes you are looking for."

> What do you sell? Repeat after me, "We sell outcomes!"

What do you sell? Repeat after me, "We sell outcomes!"

Put this phrase on your computer: "We sell outcomes!" Tape it to your dashboard. Tattoo "We sell outcomes," on the back of your hand. Put a banner up in your sales bullpen. Hire an airplane to drag a "We sell outcomes" banner in the sky in front of your office every morning.

Next, listen to what you say. When you talk to a prospect, are you talking about products you sell or outcomes you deliver? When you read your marketing material, does it start with outcomes or lead with product?

Levels of Outcomes

In the B2B space, there are four levels of outcomes you can deliver: business, risk, organizational, and personal. Each of these can be layered into your message to create compelling value propositions. Let's look at each layer.

Business Outcomes

The business outcomes are the actual bottom line results you can deliver. These typically fall into two categories: revenue growth and expenses reduction.

Every business has problems that limit their ability to make money. What problems do you solve? How does fixing these problems impact the business's ability to increase revenue or reduce expenses?

On the revenue side, how can your offering help drive revenue? Can you remove barriers to growing into new markets? Can you open new opportunities?

For example, let's say you are selling an e-commerce platform that allows local lawn and garden companies to sell their parts not just locally, but online as well. The product you sell (what you do) is an e-commerce platform. The outcome (why a buyer should care) is that you allow them to grow revenue. While you think you are selling e-commerce, what your clients are buying is a new way to sell more.

On the expense reduction side, how can your company's offering help your prospects reduce their expenses? This could be a hard cost reduction in what they are currently spending. Or, the cost reduction could be from increased efficiency.

What if you sell a cloud-based phone system that provides phone extensions to workers no matter where they are located? This system might cost more per month than the prospect is currently spending. However, if these phones enable them to transition to a home office-based workforce, this investment could save the company hundreds of thousands of dollars a year. The product you sell (what you do) is a cloud-based phone system. The outcome (why a buyer should care) is that you cut costs by enabling work-at-home opportunities.

Business outcomes should always connect to the financial statements. As they say in the south, there are only two ways to make more profit: you either raise the bridge or you lower the water. You either help increase revenue or you reduce expenses. If you do either of these, you will affect profit. Your business outcomes should always connect to profit.

Over the years, I have worked with many salespeople and read many pieces of marketing material. It always shocked me how rarely we go all the way and connect our benefit to the financial statements. That same rep that says business owners want to make more money will lead with their product instead of the outcome: making more money. Instead of making the outcomes the headline, marketing materials drone on about the wonderful feature set of the product.

When you lead with the business outcomes you deliver, you create a clear message that resonates with your prospect.

Darrell Amy

I want you to pause right now. Put yourself in the seat of your clients. How do your products and services help them increase revenue and/or reduce costs? List as many outcomes as you can think of for each of these areas.

INCREASE REVENUE	REDUCE COSTS

Risk Outcomes

In addition to increasing revenue and reducing expenses, buyers also consider risk. Every action in business comes with risk. A business owner can spend years of their life building a business and lose it in an instant. Because of this, one of the most powerful outcomes you can deliver is risk reduction.

Take the insurance industry, for example. They may think they sell insurance policies, but what clients actually buy is risk reduction. In the case of life insurance, for a small monthly premium, I remove the risk that my family will not have the financial resources they need if I die. With car insurance, I reduce the risk that I will have to pay out tens or hundreds of thousands of dollars to fix my car along with someone else's in case of an accident. I have similar insurance

REDUCE RISK - CYBER SECURITY

for my health that reduces the risk that I will go bankrupt should I get a serious disease.

I am happy to pay these premiums because I do not want the risk. The outcome I purchased was risk reduction. The product that gave me what I wanted was an insurance policy. A smart insurance company will build their message around the reduction of risk since this is the outcome their buyers want.

How can your products or services reduce your prospect's risks? Let's say you sell a payroll service. Having employees in multiple locations increases the risk that you might forget to file or pay taxes to a state or local entity. This could result in significant fines. The payroll service has experience in every state and even guarantees their work. The service you are selling (what you do) is a payroll service. One powerful outcome from your service (why a buyer would talk to you) is that you reduce their risk.

Cyber security is one of the biggest risks that companies face these days. Many products and services offer the ability to reduce these risks. Some companies sell network monitoring. Others sell products that have built-in security protocols. In either case, the outcome they are selling is reduced risk of a cyber-attack.

When you reduce a prospect's risk, you create a valuable business outcome. Pause right now and take a few moments to list the ways your product or service helps reduce your clients' risk.

REDUCE RISK

Organizational Outcomes

Abraham Maslow's famous work, *Motivation and Personality*, outlined the hierarchy of needs. The overall point of his research is that people do things for multiple reasons. Once you have the issues of survival and safety taken care of, things like love, belonging, esteem, and self-actualization come into play.

In the context of outcomes, improving profitability and reducing risk are foundational, but there are more outcomes you can consider. For example, how can you improve the organization?

Every company has employees and clients. When these two groups are happy, business goes well. When either group is dissatisfied, business becomes a challenge.

Employee satisfaction is important. Beyond the raw productivity increases we discussed in the business outcomes section above, satisfied employees are more loyal, work harder, and bring more creativity to the job. Therefore, how can your product or service improve employee satisfaction?

Let's say that you sell semi-trucks (lorries for my European friends). Your trucks include the industry's most comfortable seat with air-conditioning vents and a built-in massage system. The product (what you sell) is a truck. The outcome (why the prospect should talk to you) is improved employee satisfaction. After all, what other trucking companies give their employees a massage as they drive down the road? This leads to happier drivers and lower turnover. What is nice about this outcome is that it will filter to the bottom line since turnover can be expensive.

Client satisfaction is critical as well. If clients are not happy, then a business will struggle. This will filter down to employees that face the unpleasant task of dealing with unhappy clients. How can your product or service improve client satisfaction?

If you sell a cloud-based platform for financial planners, then one of the challenges their clients face is not knowing how their multiple investments are performing. As a result, clients are always calling and emailing to ask for updates, wondering how their net worth is growing. Your cloud-based platform aggregates a client's investment performance into one secure portal. Your product (what you sell) is a cloud-based platform for financial planners. Your outcome (why a prospect would

87

talk with you) is better client satisfaction. Of course, this also filters down to the bottom line through increased client retention.

What outcomes can you deliver related to employee satisfaction and client satisfaction? Invest a few minutes to brainstorm and list these below.

EMPLOYEE SATISFACTION	CLIENT SATISFACTION

Personal Outcomes

People buy from people. That means that your buyers likely have a personal interest in the decision.

If you are talking with a business owner, they are by default personally involved in their business because they are the business. Your product or service will affect them personally along with their family.

> Consider the personal outcomes your clients and prospects want.

Consider the personal outcomes your clients and prospects want. If you sell to small business owners, maybe they want to leave a legacy for their children. How can you help them leave a legacy? Could your recommendation help them successfully pass the business to the next generation or could it help streamline their exit plan?

I know of an ERP (Enterprise Resource Planning) company that sells accounting and operations software to a niche market. The primary outcome that their buyers want is to be able to sell their business. They know that if they adopt this ERP platform, it will make it easy for their business to be integrated into a larger business after the purchase. The product (what you sell) is an ERP system. The outcome (why they would give you attention) is that it facilitates a smooth sale, giving the owner an exit plan. This company could have the greatest feature set in the world, but when it comes down to the decision, the thing motivating the purchase is simply the owner's exit strategy.

If you are selling to a business manager, someone that does not own the business, there are personal implications as well. Whether the decision-maker is a CEO appointed by the board of directors or a general manager hired by a company owner, this person has personal skin in the game. If their decisions make the company profitable and reduce risk while improving client and employee satisfaction, they likely have job security. If they make a decision that harms the company, their career could be in jeopardy.

The outcome a business manager wants is increased prestige, income, promotion, and job security. Most of them also want to be liked by their team.

Let's say you are a commercial real estate broker leasing office space. The product (what you sell) is office space with a nicer corner office, a better employee lounge, and space to grow. The outcome (why they would talk to you) is career advancement by offering more prestige and admiration from happy employees.

What personal outcomes can you deliver to business owners or managers? List these below.

PERSONAL OUTCOMES

Share Your Message

With your outcomes in mind, it is time to share your message, which needs to be consistent and flow seamlessly through all your buyer and client interactions. Now it is time to consider how to share this message in your marketing and sales materials.

Important Points

1. What business are you in? When you get this answer right, everything comes into focus.

2. Buyers do not buy products; they buy outcomes.

3. There are four levels of outcomes: business, risk, organizational, and personal.

Chapter 5: Build an Outcomes Inventory

The last chapter began with a tasty description of how delicious maple syrup is made by boiling sap. Another similar product that needs to be refined is gasoline. Gasoline begins as crude oil. This thick, black substance contains the energy to power your car.

If you tried to put crude oil into your engine, you would not get very far. You would destroy your engine. Crude oil must be refined down to a fuel we call gasoline. Only then is it able to power an engine.

Your company's message works the same way. It needs to be refined. When it is, you will not only deliver something appealing and delicious to your prospects, but you will also have created the fuel you need to power your Revenue Growth Engine.

While the fuel of your clear message makes your Revenue Growth Engine run, the opposite holds true. If you do not take the time to refine your message, you can have the most powerful engine in the world, but without good fuel, it will not perform. You will be looking at your marketing and sales enablement efforts and wondering why you are not getting results.

> The way to distill your marketing message into powerful fuel for your Revenue Growth Engine is by focusing on the outcomes that your prospects and clients want.

The way to distill your marketing message into powerful fuel for your Revenue Growth Engine is by focusing on the outcomes that your prospects and clients want. This will guarantee that your marketing message will be appealing to your prospects and clients, helping you get the attention you need. Since most of your competition markets their products, not their outcomes, developing an outcomes-based message will also build your competitive advantage.

What Outcomes Do Your Prospects Value?

Prospects do not buy products or services—they buy outcomes. How do you determine what outcomes your prospects value? The best way to find out is to ask current clients.

Marketing professionals: instead of sitting in our offices segmenting our prospects, we need to get out into the real world and engage with them. Marketing gurus Clay Christensen, Scott Cook, and Taddy Hall tell the story of the Sony Walkman. Sony founder, Akio Morita, was a wise man who sent his marketing team out to search for the outcomes his customers wanted. They discovered that the market wanted the ability to take music with them while escaping the world. This understanding of the desired outcome led to the creation of the Walkman and the rest is history.

To create fuel for your Revenue Growth Engine, you need to understand the outcomes your prospects desire. Here are three practical ways you can do this.

Field Rides

Christensen, Cook, and Hall recommend you learn from the story of the Walkman: "Turn off the computer, get out of the office, and observe!"[vi]

Most marketing people never leave the office. As a marketing professional, I recommend that you invest one day each month with your sales team. If you have a field sales team, go on sales calls and client visits with them. This time will be invaluable because you will hear the challenges that prospects and clients face.

Take good notes. Listen for challenges and concerns. These will be the keywords that you will use later in your marketing messages.

Pay close attention to what your sales reps are saying. How does that align with your clear message? If your sales team works over the phone or through Web meetings, sit in on their meetings. Listen closely to the conversations. Take special notes of the questions that prospects are asking.

Success Stories

Success stories, also known as case studies, can be a powerful tool you can use to fuel your clear message and enable your sales team. These stories contain the gold nuggets of insight into why your clients buy, what made them choose your company, and how they use your products. The things you learn in a case study will define your message.

Sadly, most companies put writing or recording success stories at the bottom of the list when it comes to their marketing. I have seen it happen repeatedly. They say things such as, "We just need a website and do not have time to handle all of these case studies." As a result, they end up publishing another me-too product-centered website that does not resonate with their prospects or differentiate themselves from the competition. Success stories become the can that gets kicked down the street and forgotten.

> When buyers hear stories about other companies that you have helped with their product, they are able to see the outcomes.

Similarly, salespeople do not feel like they have the time to contact clients to arrange for interviews. After all, they are busy banging the phones to get appointments and trying to close business sales to hit their quotas. What salespeople need to realize is that if their message was focused on what clients want, they'd be able to get more appointments and close more business sales.

CASE HISTORIES
SUCCESS STORIES

Stories sell. When you can tell a real-world story, two things happen. First, you make complex concepts simple. The product or service that you sell may be very complicated. Complexity makes buyers shut down. However, when buyers hear stories about other companies that you have helped with their product, they are able to see the outcomes.

Second, when you tell an honest story from a client you have served, you build trust. We work in a post-trust era. "Misinformation" was Dictionary.com's 2018 word of the year. With fake news and false advertising on the rise, buyers are more skeptical than ever. Success stories help break down the walls of mistrust by featuring real clients telling their stories about how they benefit from your offerings.

I believe that the Number One role of marketing should be to interview current clients and write success stories. Why? Everything rides on the knowledge you get from your clients:

- The message that flows through your website, social media, and printed material will be effective.

- The way your salespeople prospect, present, and close will be more compelling when they lead with stories of how other companies benefitted.

I recommend that you start with success stories before you do any work on your website, create a sales presentation, or do anything related to your company message.

If you are a marketing professional, you should set a target of writing at least one success story every month. If you currently do not have any success stories, I would recommend writing one a week for the next 90 days. By doing this, you will have an overwhelmingly powerful library of insights that you can use to create your marketing message.

How do you write or record a success story? It is easy. You begin with an overview of the client and their business. You talk about the challenges they faced. Then, you show what your company did to solve their problems. Finally, you end by itemizing the outcomes (or benefits) they enjoy. Throughout the success story, you can sprinkle the juicy pull-quotes.

Ideally, success stories should be in both written and video formats. Since video takes time and a budget, I recommend starting with written case studies that can be shared on your website and used by your sales team. Then, find the clients that seem to be the best fit for the camera and send in a video crew.

If you would like some guidance on how to structure your story to minimize the amount of time required by a client, I have put together a guide on creating great success stories. You can find it at **www.RevenueGrowthEngine.net/free-tool-kit.**

Do not skip this step. Most companies will gloss over writing success stories. This is the key to refining the message that will fuel your Revenue Growth Engine.

Take People to Lunch

In addition to going out in the field and writing success stories, I recommend doing some qualitative market research.

You do not need to spend tens of thousands of dollars on focus groups and surveys. Instead, I recommend taking people to lunch and asking questions.

Years ago, I launched a vertical market initiative to help my clients understand how to sell their technology to various industries. I noticed that most of the vertical market information was product centered. Technology companies had started with their product and tried to shoe-horn it into various verticals, combining their technical jargon with the lingo of each industry. The result was unproductive.

Instead, my approach was to begin with outcomes, not products. The first market I targeted was the mortgage industry. Since my clients sold document management solutions, I wanted to understand how information flowed from the time someone applied for a mortgage until the deal closed.

At that time, I was refinancing my home, so I called my mortgage broker and asked if I could buy him lunch. During the meal, I asked him about the challenges he was facing in the industry. I then asked what happened with a mortgage application after I applied for a loan.

At the end of the lunch, I not only left with a full stomach, I had a full notepad of insight into the current "on-the-street" challenges of a mortgage broker. I also learned how their business worked and where the real problems were.

After this, I replicated my work by talking to a friend who was a litigation coordinator for a large law firm in Dallas. Then, I interviewed the office administrator for the medical clinic that would deliver my first child. Over the next year, I leveraged my network of friends to talk with people in key verticals.

For the price of a meal or a box of bagels, you can get inside the mind of your prospective clients. You begin to understand the outcomes they desire. You get an inside look into the challenges they face. All of this can be used to create fuel for the clear message that will power your Revenue Growth Engine.

Just like I recommend that marketing professionals spend one day a month in the field and write one case study a month, I suggest that you take someone to lunch once a week with the goal of listening to understand their business.

Create Your Outcomes Inventory

Most companies have an inventory of products sitting in a warehouse. The problem is that buyers do not buy products, they buy outcomes. Therefore, you need to create an inventory of outcomes. These outcomes will become the foundation for your clear message.

Now that you have ridden in the field, written some success stories, and bought a few lunches, you are ready to craft your value proposition. This is simply a list of ways that your company can help prospects achieve outcomes.

Itemize Your Outcomes Inventory

Start by making a list of the outcomes you deliver. For each outcome, think about what it means to your client and their business. Just like the maple syrup we talked about in the last chapter, you are boiling down everything you learned into a master list. This should fit on one or two pages. This value document is priceless.

Back Up the Outcomes with Proof

Next, you need to back up each of your value claims. This step is critical. "An offering may actually provide superior value—but if the supplier does not demonstrate and document that claim, a customer manager will likely dismiss it as marketing puffery."[vii]

How do you get past the puffery? Success stories are a good start. They give you direct quotes from clients that claim they have received value.

In addition to client quotes, look for real data to back up your claims. For example, if your clients tell you that they value one hour or less service response time in an industry known to normally take a day, pull data on your average service response time over the past year. If you claim that your offering helps accounting firms cut the time it takes to prepare a tax return, back that up with a success story and some real-world data.

You can also connect the features of your products and services to outcomes. For example, if you sell delivery truck fleets to buyers that value the outcome of "reducing driver injuries," then you can connect features like your automatic liftgate or fold-out entry step.

Darrell Amy

Always be on the lookout for ways to substantiate your claims. Add the supporting client quotes and data to your outcomes inventory.

For an outcomes inventory worksheet, visit

www.RevenueGrowthEngine.net/free-tool-kit

Categorize Your Statements by Decision-Maker

Next, categorize your outcome statements by your core decision-makers and influencers. Brent Adamson and Matt Dixon's research presented in *The Challenger Customer* revealed that the average B2B buying decision involved 6.7 people. Chances are that each of these decision-makers and influencers have different priorities. Decision-makers may value different aspects of your offering.

Think about your clients. If you sell to a business environment, there will usually be a finance decision-maker, an operational decision-maker, and possibly an information technology decision-maker. You also have the owner or executive, as well as some end users. Let's take a moment and consider what each of these people value:

- **Owners/Executives:** Concerned about future growth of the company.

- **Finance:** Concerned about expense management and profitability.

- **Information Technology:** Concerned about security and integration with their current systems.

- **Operations:** Concerned about how it affects the way they do things.

Now, think about the decision-makers and influencers in your industry. What do each of them value? Next, look at your value list. Which items on your value list apply to each decision-maker? It is okay if one of your value items applies to more than one decision-maker. The key is to recognize that what one person considers valuable may not mean a lot to the other influencer.

Consider Your Competition

The final step is to understand what differentiates you from your competition. We all have competitors. Many of them are good companies that sell similar products to yours and deliver good services. In this environment where everyone is saying the same thing, your prospects tend to see the competition as the same. When this happens, you slip into commodity status and decisions get made on price.

Look at your value list. Based on what you know about your competition, where do you stand out? What things do your prospects value that you can do better and back up with supporting data?

Earlier, we talked about maple syrup. In the process of making maple syrup, something very special happens. Around the edges, sugar-like crystals form from super-distilled sap. This is called maple sugar. If you have ever tasted this, it tastes like heaven.

The unique ways you stand out from the competition are like high-performance racing fuel. In a world where much of your competition is saying the same thing, you will be able to communicate value that resonates. This is hard work, but the end result will be a clear message to fuel your Revenue Growth Engine.

In the next chapter, we will explore how to share a clear message across your marketing. Then, we will look at how to apply the same clear message to your sales materials.

Important Points

1. Since buyers buy outcomes, not products, you need an inventory of outcomes that you sell.

2. You create this inventory by listening to clients:

    *   Go on field rides.

    *   Write success stories.

    *   Take clients to lunch.

3. Create your outcomes inventory:

    *   List all the outcomes you deliver.

    *   Identify which decision-makers and influencers value these outcomes.

    *   Back it up with success stories, quotes, features, and data.

Darrell Amy

Chapter 6: Focus Your Marketing Message

Picture yourself on a Friday night, snuggled up next to your significant other to watch a romantic comedy. In that movie, you are likely to see a bad date scene. The outcome is predictable. One person goes on and on about themselves, while the other person tries to make a graceful exit. Awkward!

What makes a bad date? One person who is obsessed with themselves and dominates the conversation. Everything is about them. The other person sits there bored, and you can feel the tension as they struggle to find a way to leave.

Fortunately, in our world of online dating websites, you can filter out many of the self-absorbed candidates before you get to the awkward date. These are the profiles where people talk about how great they are, flexing their muscles, flaunting their possessions, and fawning over their accomplishments.

How do you feel about a person like that? You hit the back button or swipe to the next profile! After all, who wants to date a self-absorbed narcissist?

While this book is not about dating, there are parallels to creating a clear message. It is like your business is dating your prospective clients. Sales professionals that only talk about how great they are will repulse buyers. Marketing messages that lead with the greatness of the company and the products get the same reaction that the self-promoting narcissist gets on a dating website: "Next!"

Zig Ziglar was famous for saying, "You will get all you want in life, if you help enough other people get what they want." Your focused message should focus on helping your target market achieve its outcomes. It is like being the courteous person on the date that listens. Goodwill is generated when you talk about what is essential to the other person.

In the last chapter, we explored how to create a clear message by focusing on what your clients and prospects desire. Your outcome-based message fuels your Revenue Growth Engine. Most marketing messages do not begin with outcomes. Unfortunately, they lead with flowery descriptions of the company's long history, responsive service, and robust product line.

Over the years, I have reviewed the marketing messages of hundreds of companies. The majority of them read like this: "Me, me, me, me, me, me...you." It is all about the company. Sometimes, near the bottom of the page, they might get around to talking about how the client benefits.

Your marketing content should read like this: "You, you, you, you, you...US!" Lead with the client's desired outcome and then conclude with ways you could work with them to accomplish it.

When prospects or clients read or watch any of your marketing messages, they should immediately get the sense that, "This company understands me." You want your prospects to think that your company is the best choice. The way to make this happen is by talking about the client's desired outcomes.

In this chapter, we will talk about how to take your focused message and present it across all your marketing platforms: website, social media, advertising, emails, and even your office. In the next chapter, we will look at how to craft a focused sales message.

Website

Your website anchors your focused message. For many businesses, only a handful of prospects and clients ever visit their office. Yet they spend tens of thousands of dollars on the facilities. Their offices may have plush conference room furniture, beautiful decorations, and immaculate landscaping, but these same companies go cheap when it comes to their website.

Do not cut corners on your website. An excellent website gives credibility to your business. Viewers will judge you by the quality they see there. Invest the time and money to make sure that the content and the visuals on your website resonate with clients and prospects.

Your website needs to get an "A" in both style and substance. Both are important. You need it to look appropriate because that is where first impressions form. Beyond the first impression of style, your website must have substance. Let's explore each of these.

Style

Buyers form first impressions based on your online brand. To continue the dating analogy, if you show up for a first date to a fine restaurant in a ripped t-shirt and gym shorts, your first impression will not get you a second date. Your website needs to be styled in a way that makes a great first impression.

What is an appropriate style for your website? Style is personal. Some website styles feel current and professional; other designs feel cheap and even cartoonish.

Website styles are like fashion trends. That light blue polyester three-piece suit with a plaid vest and white tie looked great in the 1970s, but it would be out of place now. The website built ten years ago seems out of style today. Whether you like it or not, out-of-style sites leave the wrong impression, making you look dated, sloppy, or even worse, incompetent.

How do you determine current website styles? You do this the same way that you discover fashion trends. To find out what to wear, you pick up a magazine or catalog and look at what the brands you love are wearing. I am not much of a fashionista, but as a businessperson, I know that I can look to leading brands like Calvin Klein and Johnston and Murphy to see what is "in."

To determine current website styles, look at what the big brands are doing. If you are in technology, go to the websites of Apple, HP, Dell, IBM, and Cisco. Notice how they are "digitally dressed." While you may not have the marketing budget of these companies, you can get a sense of what is current and emulate it.

As you design your website, make sure to consider the devices your prospects use to view your site. Smart web designers use "mobile-first" designs. They recognize that most visitors will see their company on a tiny screen. Mobile devices have flipped web design on its head. We used to design for big monitors first; now we design for small mobile screens first.

Fifteen years ago, when we built a website for a client, we focused on the slideshow on the home page. The goal was to bedazzle the visitor with slides that showcased everything the company did. When slideshows were new, this worked well. As people started adopting mobile devices, we noticed two things. First, the vast majority of people never made it past the first slide. Second, since the slide show had a lot of images, it took longer for the page to load. Impatient mobile visitors gave up waiting. Google's mobile-first search results ended up pushing these websites down in the search rankings, hurting traffic.

Even with this evidence that slideshows are out of style on the home page, we still have companies that insist on using them on their new websites. Others do not see the need to update their old website, even though it makes them look dated.

111

These companies end up looking like the dad that shows up to a wedding in that old light blue polyester suit.

Substance

While style is essential for the first impression, your website visitors' attention quickly turns to the substance. Within the first few seconds of coming to your website, visitors must be able to immediately understand what your company does.

> If a caveman visited your website, they should be able to say, "Me want widget. This company sells widget."

Donald Miller, the author of *Building a StoryBrand*, calls this "passing the grunt test."

If a caveman visited your website, they should be able to say, "Me want widget. This company sells widget."

I have watched many companies get too clever when building a website. By the time they are done, their website is beautiful, but nobody understands what they do. Make sure your visitors can quickly see what you do, so they know they are in the right place.

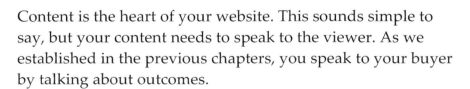

Content is the heart of your website. This sounds simple to say, but your content needs to speak to the viewer. As we established in the previous chapters, you speak to your buyer by talking about outcomes.

Look at most websites, and you will find content written to the owner of the company, not the prospective client. They are filled with endless pages of self-congratulation and history about the company.

I am proud that your company has been around for "287 years" and has won all kinds of "industry awards." I'm glad that you have an "experienced team" that "prides itself on delivering outstanding service." Just be careful. Too much self-congratulation and you'll end up creating the bad date scene we talked about at the beginning of the chapter. If the buyer wants to make a swift exit, all they need to do is click the back button!

The accolades of your company are relevant to your visitors after they get a sense that you understand their world and can help them achieve their outcomes. First, visitors want to know what outcomes you deliver. The outcomes you provide should be front and center on the website.

In *Building a StoryBrand*, Donald Miller asserts that we should look at the message on our website like we look at the script for a good movie. Every movie has a hero. In the screenplay of your company, the hero is not you; it is the prospect! That hero meets a guide that helps them solve their problems and find success. You want to be the guide. Make the prospect and their success the focus of your website, and you will shine like a star among all your self-congratulating competitors.[viii]

Most of today's websites call the main section at the top of the page the "hero banner." That is an excellent name because the message should focus on the hero and the outcomes you can deliver to them.

Let's say you have a janitorial services company. If you make yourself the hero, the headline on the home page might say, "Janitorial services since 1959." In the background, you might have a picture of your office building. As you go down the page, you'd talk about your awards and the cleaning products you use. You might also have a few client references. This is a setup for a bad date!

If you took the approach of making your prospect the hero, your message then becomes about the outcomes you offer. In the success story interviews you did with your top clients, you learned that what they valued most was how they felt like they were getting a competitive advantage from the Five Star Detail Process and the way you took care of them. This approach helped them attract more business.

Armed with this insight about the outcomes your clients desire, here are some headline options:

- Build Your Competitive Advantage with a Five Star Facility

- Wow Your Prospects, Clients, and Employees from the Moment They Open Your Door

- Maintain Your Professional Image to Support Your Growth

To reinforce that the client is the hero, you could feature an image of your ideal client. Maybe it is a 50-year old businesswoman smiling with a clean office in the background, or maybe you could display pictures of the offices of some of your key clients. Make your prospect the hero, and you increase your chances of getting a second date.

As you go down the home page, you can discuss how you deliver the outcomes. You have a video describing your Five Star Detail Process. Success studies and references showcase how other local companies have benefitted. Finally, you call the buyer to action with a Five Star Detail for their lobby and conference room.

Here is a common problem we see with most websites. Beyond the home page, the content lacks depth. The internal pages are weak.

The problem with weak internal content is twofold. First, many people that find your company in a Google search do not come in through the home page since the result sends them directly to the internal page that provides content on the specific topic of the search. This person misses the home page entirely. That means internal pages need to stand on their own.

The second problem with shallow content is that visitors may be impressed with the home page, but when they click to an internal page, they are underwhelmed. One click of the back button and they are gone.

What type of content should be in the internal pages of your website? Buyers come to your website with questions. If they find helpful answers to their inquiries, they stay. If they do not, they hit the back button and go to another company's website. It is that simple.

One technology company that our team serviced noticed a website visitor spent three hours reading fifty-seven pages on their website. This visitor consumed content from their blog and several product pages. The very next day, someone else from the same company filled out a form on the website and requested a meeting. The opportunity resulted in a good-sized net-new sale.

After the sale, the sales rep asked the decision-maker about the visits to the website. It turns out that the decision-maker delegated the role of research to a younger employee. That employee did their homework. Not surprisingly, she recommended the vendor with the most helpful web content.

 In his book, *They Ask, You Answer*, Marcus Sheridan recommends that companies consider the questions that buyers might have related to their products and services. These questions form the foundation for the content on the website.

Search engines are essentially answering machines that serve up answers to questions buyers have. When your website answers these questions, you develop placement in Google.

As you move into the sales cycle, buyers have questions while they are evaluating alternatives. These days, it is not uncommon for a buyer to be searching on the Internet while they are talking to a salesperson. Why does this happen? Buyers are skeptical. In a post-trust era, they are looking to validate everything salespeople say.

> Buyers are skeptical. In a post-trust era, they are looking to validate everything salespeople say.

After the sale, your clients will also look at your website. They have questions about support. While you may think that "answering the phone with a live human being" is the essence of excellent support, many of today's clients do not want to pick up the phone. They would rather find the answers to their support questions online. The more support content you can put on your website, the better your level of support and the lower your support costs.

Your clients will also come to your website in response to cross-sell campaigns that promote additional products and services you sell. When they click on a link from that email, they need to find enough content about your new product or service to make them feel comfortable that you know what you're doing in this new area. This client trusts you for your core business, but they may not feel as confident with your abilities in your new product or service area. The job of your website is to alleviate their fears.

Blog

Blog articles are a core component of today's websites. It is where you can answer questions your buyers have about your products and services. As you get questions from your clients and prospects, answer them on your blog.

Blog articles can also explain your business philosophy. Write articles about why you are in business. Explain what you

believe. Write about your thoughts on your industry. This helps buyers feel the personality of your company.

Over time, you will create a library of content that helps your buyers find answers to their questions while understanding your company. Search engines love this content. So do smart salespeople who can send buyers links to articles that answer questions instead of having to type long email responses.

The blog is also where you establish thought leadership as a provider. In their book, *Insight Selling*, Mike Schultz and John Doerr present research from extensive buyer interviews. The main things buyers want from salespeople is insight: "Sales winners educate with new ideas and perspectives almost three times more often than second-place finishers. Of 42 factors studied, the greatest difference between winners and second-place finishers was their propensity to educate."[ix]

If sales reps are going to educate their prospects, the primary source of ideas should come from your company. When it comes to driving revenue, your blog is so important. Do not slack on your blog. Make sure you capture insights from your company's thought leaders.

Beyond supporting sales, blogs also form the foundation for your outreach. On social media, you can share articles. Blogs will form the foundation of your client email campaigns. Blogs also provide great content for search engines to index, as we will discuss in a later chapter.

While establishing credibility is vital across all areas of your business, it is essential when it comes to new areas of your business. As we discussed above, your market knows and trusts you for your core products. When you add new products and services, it takes time to build awareness and trust in these new areas.

Over the past few years, I have had the opportunity to work with office equipment companies that wanted to build managed network services businesses. It turned out that the clients that trusted them to work on their copiers and printers did not necessarily trust the company to manage their network, data, and security. The smart companies used their website and blog to publish articles, positioning them as network support experts. Over time, the consistent message began to boost trust, enabling more clients to come on board.

> Do this consistently over a year and you will create a powerful body of information to fuel the growth of your business.

Plan to add at least one blog article to your website a week. If you are just getting started, you may want to add two or three articles a week. Do this consistently over a year and you will create a powerful body of information to fuel the growth of your business.

How long should blog articles be? Ask five people and you will get five different answers. My response is that they should be long enough to answer the question. Whether that is 350 words or 3,500 words, the point is to help your buyer.

Darrell Amy

Social Media

Social media also plays a vital role in fueling your Revenue Growth Engine. However, I believe that many companies have invested too much focus on this area while neglecting the core components of the growth engine.

Social media amplifies your message. If you do not have the right message (that is, helpful and engaging content on your website and blog), then your social media will be a flop. As Larry Levine, author of *Selling from the Heart,* says, "You end up becoming an empty suit. You look good, but underneath you have no substance."

Social media creates awareness while building your brand. Your social media posts should be a mix of sharing your culture and showing your competence.

Culture posts include people; they are the faces of your company. We know that social media platforms will continue to grow and evolve, so I hesitate to put too much detail about them in the book. However, as of the writing of this book, platforms like Facebook, Instagram, Pinterest, and Snapchat provide the best forums to build the cultural side of your business.

Social media also plays the role of building the online personality of your company. Before you discount this too much, remember what Bob Burg, author of *The Go-Giver*, says, "All things being equal, people will do business with and refer business to, those people they know, like, and trust."

In the context of presenting a clear message to fuel your Revenue Growth Engine, it is beneficial to position your company as a team of friendly, helpful, and trustworthy people. Social media can help do this.

One client we worked with provided serious B2B technology services. Most of their social media presence was on LinkedIn and Twitter. However, some of their core influencers were office managers. They were primarily females in their 40s and 50s. After talking to a few of them, we discovered that they loved Pinterest. Our team wrote that off until we noticed the new company cookbook sitting on the table in the reception area. We took recipes from the cookbook and put them on Pinterest. Guess what? The office managers loved it. It built trust, helping them feel comfortable recommending the company for technology services.

In addition to building culture, social media should reinforce competence. LinkedIn has become the suit and tie business network and is the place where you want to share thought-leadership articles. On this platform, your company can build top-of-mind awareness and credibility by sharing blog articles that provide helpful strategies.

When it comes to building competence, shy away from sharing pictures of your products. Instead, share helpful articles. Remember to focus content on the outcomes that are important to your buyers. If you sell to businesses, your posts might include articles about business strategy, trends, or solutions to common problems. To sell to individuals, you want to share articles that help people improve their lives.

Social media also provides new ways to interact with potential buyers. In the net-new business section, we will talk about how you can leverage this to drive opportunities. If you want this interaction to generate leads, you need to be active in sharing content on your social media platforms.

Email

Email is the acid test for the effectiveness of your message. It is more critical to present a clear message led by outcomes in your emails than anywhere else.

Clients and buyers move quickly through their inboxes. I think Jon Ferrara, inventor of the first CRM, Goldmine, and the founder of Nimble, put it best: "My inbox is a slaughterhouse!"

You create the subject line for the outcome your client wants, or they will ignore your emails, they will click unsubscribe, or you will get relegated to their junk folders. Emails get used throughout the buyer's journey and client experience. We will explore specific uses of email throughout this book as we look at each stage of your Revenue Growth Engine. In this section, let's think high-level about the message itself.

Email messages must be relevant to the recipient. How do you ensure the email is relevant? Focus the content on outcomes they desire, not on your products or company. Outcomes should be front and center in your subject line and the first few sentences of your email.

If the first few words of your subject line do not point to an outcome, then rewrite it. For example, if your headline says,

"ABC Company Helps Deliver Faster Accounts Payable Processing," then flip the headline to something like, "New Faster Accounts Payable Processing Solution." If you think about it, you do not even need to put your company name in the headline because it is already in the From field.

Personalize the message as much as possible. In the Revenue Growth Engine model, sales reps launch one-to-one emails to prospects. You will learn how to use templates and sequences to make it easy for sales reps to customize template messages, providing a consistent company message while allowing sales reps to customize. The content in the email templates should focus on outcomes.

Send bulk emails to only the clients and people who have signed up for one of your lists. Even in bulk emails, you should always look for ways to segment your list and customize your content to the recipients.

Resist the urge to use gimmicks. Yesterday, I received a promotional email from a large electronics retailer. They used a blue circle emoticon at the beginning of the subject line so that it would look like the message was unread even after I had opened it. That's an easy reason for a recipient to unsubscribe.

If you focus on creating outcomes-based content in all these areas, then your Revenue Growth Engine will avoid the bad first date scenarios we discussed at the beginning of this chapter, and it will lead to many long and happy client relationships!

Important Points

1. Look at your website, social media, and other marketing collateral through the lens of your ideal buyer and the outcomes they want. Does it resonate? What do you see? What do you need to change?

2. Invest the time and money to make sure that the content and the visuals on your website resonate with clients and prospects.

3. Beyond supporting sales, blogs also form the foundation for your outreach. On social media, you can share articles. Blogs will form the foundation of your client email campaigns. Blogs also provide great content for search engines to index.

4. Social media creates awareness while building your brand. Your social media posts should be a mix of sharing your culture and showing your competence.

5. Email is the acid test for the effectiveness of your message. It is more critical to present a clear message led by outcomes in your emails than anywhere else.

Chapter 7: Focus Your Sales Message

My wife and I are buying a new home. Truthfully, we do not want to buy a home. Buying a home is a huge hassle that requires a scary financial transaction, the challenge of selling our current home, and the work of moving.

While we do not want to go through the hassle of relocating, what we do want are outcomes:

- We want to spend more time with our grandchildren, so we want a pool.

- I want to enjoy my woodworking hobby without taking over our garage for weeks on end, so I want a shop.

- I want to do more writing, so I am interested in a peaceful place in the country instead of living in town.

- I want to record more videos, so I am looking for a dark room where I can set up a green screen.

- I want to reduce our expenses, so I like the idea that my wife can move her photography studio from a rented commercial space to our property.

I do not want to buy a house. I certainly do not want to pack and move! But I do want these outcomes.

I have met many real estate agents over the past few months. I am shocked at how many never ask me about the outcomes I desire. Instead, they focus on the product—in this case, the house. They feature the square footage and other specs. They talk about the great view, the location, and the schools, but very few have asked me why I am moving.

Imagine how effective the real estate agents would be if they asked what outcomes I wanted. Instead of talking about square footage, they could show me a place where I would hang out with my grandkids, work in a shop, write a book, and record video while allowing my wife's studio to be on the property.

As wonderful as your products are, and as great as your company is, buyers do not buy your products, they buy outcomes.

Talking about the outcome that clients desire will get their attention. The more you can remember that buyers buy outcomes and not products, the more effective your sales message will be. In this chapter, we will explore how to communicate outcomes throughout the sales process.

Elevator Pitch

Every salesperson needs to deliver their elevator pitch at a moment's notice. What do you say when someone asks, "What do you do?" The usual response is to answer with your product or service:

- I sell employee benefits and payroll services.

- I sell commercial real estate.

- I sell delivery services to manufacturers.

Notice that most of these responses begin with, "I sell" and continue with a description of the product.

What if you flipped the script and shared the outcomes you deliver instead of the product? The answer to "What do you do?" could be:

- I help companies drive employee satisfaction and reduce their tax risks.

- I help retail stores find locations that drive traffic and grow revenue.

- I help manufacturing companies fulfill their delivery promises and reduce warehouse operation expenses.

Notice that these sentences begin with "I help" instead of "I sell." They focus on the outcome, not the product.

Most business decisions involve multiple decision-makers in various roles. You customize your elevator pitches to the outcomes desired by the person you are speaking with. For example, you sell a managed network services program that monitors computer networks. Here are some elevator pitches to various decision-makers:

- I help IT directors reduce network downtime and manage security risks.

Darrell Amy

- I help CFOs lower tech support costs while creating a predictable budget.

- I help department managers keep their employees happy and productive.

In all three cases, the product is the same: a managed network services program. By customizing the outcomes to what is important to each decision-maker, you express your value in a way that captures attention.

To create your elevator pitch, go back to the outcomes inventory you created. You should be able to find a treasure-trove of ideas.

To help you get started, you can use this simple framework:

*I help (<u>functional role and vertical market</u>) (**insert outcomes here**).*

Here are some examples to the "What do you do?" question:

- I help <u>CFOs of healthcare companies</u> **reduce malpractice risk while improving patient care**.

- I help <u>manufacturing companies</u> **improve quality control and reduce equipment downtime**.

- I help <u>accounting firms</u> **increase revenue by processing tax returns more efficiently during tax season**.

Do a good job with the first sentence of your elevator pitch; your prospect will then likely ask, "How do you do that?" Now you've been invited to explain what you sell.

Consider the dynamic here. When you answer the "What do you do?" question with a list of your products, you immediately jump into sales mode, trying to cram as much as you can into twenty seconds, and then asking a closing question. The buyer gets defensive and shuts you down.

When you answer, "What do you do?" with the outcomes they desire, the buyer opens up. You establish curiosity. You connect with their goals, challenges, and desires. The door opens for them to ask you how you accomplish the outcome. They ask, and you answer. The difference between the two dynamics is huge.

What could your elevator pitch be? Make a list of potential elevator pitches for various types of prospects you target. This task is a great exercise to do in your next sales meeting.

These outcome statements should be the very first thing new reps learn. In most industries, new reps will not know all there is to know about the products and services. Get them off to a good start by selling outcomes. Then they can learn the products and services as they go.

Prospecting

 Jeb Blount, the author of *Fanatical Prospecting*, says that the number one reason for empty sales funnels is the failure to prospect. Why do salespeople avoid prospecting? I believe the main reason salespeople do not prospect is that they don't know what to say. Thus, prospecting is something they see as ineffective—even though it is the source of their income.

Prospecting is about getting attention. Without attention, nothing happens. When you lead with the outcomes your prospects want, you increase your odds of capturing some attention. This attention leads to appointments and then to sales.

> Sales reps can improve their call-to-appointment ratios by leading with outcomes.

Whether you are prospecting on the phone or out in the field, prospecting is a numbers game. Much like a batter in baseball, you are going to strike out more times than you hit, but with training, a player can improve their batting average. Sales reps can improve their call-to-appointment ratios by leading with outcomes.

When we get a prospect on the phone, we tend to talk mainly about our products or services and we might say, "I'm calling today to talk about your janitorial services and how we might save you some money." Or, we ask, "Who's in charge of your office supplies?" There are two problems with this approach. First, the only people that will give you the time of day are those that are looking for janitorial services. The second problem is that when you do find someone looking for janitorial services, you have now set yourself up to not make any money. By leading with "I can save you some money," you've launched the conversation around cost—the last thing a smart sales rep wants to do.

Instead, what if you prospected using outcome statements? How about this: "I am calling today because other companies have found ways to improve their competitive advantage and employee morale." Or, "I am calling you because other local companies have found a way to reduce sick days this coming winter."

Both approaches start listing the outcomes. The first approach sets up a conversation about competitive advantage and better employee morale by having a facility that is professionally maintained. The second approach sets up an appointment about reducing sick days by making sure your office is disinfected. Either approach is much more compelling than, "I am calling to talk about your janitorial services."

Sales Collateral

During the sales process, reps send brochures and product sheets to the buyer. The consensus is that it is a waste of paper.

What if your company brochure featured the outcomes you deliver? If you took my advice earlier, you now have a library of success stories. Use excerpts from these to create a compelling company brochure. Discuss how you achieve these outcomes. Then you can feature your products and services.

Sell sheets can follow the same model. Buyers buy outcomes; sell sheets should list outcomes on the front. Then, put the specs and pricing on the back.

Sales packages can support the sales process. When you focus on outcomes, you create tools that enable your sales team to get attention, build value, and win deals.

Presentations

The world is in the midst of a sleep crisis, with an increasing number of people suffering from insomnia. I have a solution to the sleep crisis. Most people's insomnia could be instantly cured by attending a sales presentation.

Think back to sales presentations you have seen (or delivered). How many of them began with a stack of slides about the history of the company and the products?

I'm not saying that your company's history, experienced staff, and amazing service or product are unimportant, but a prospect is selfish and wants to know what it will do for them.

> Rather than lead your next presentation with the history of the company, what if you talked about the outcomes you have delivered for other similar companies?

Rather than lead your next presentation with the history of the company, what if you talked about the outcomes you have delivered for other similar companies? What if you shared the ways that you can help deliver results that are important to the buyer?

I remember delivering one of my most successful sales presentations to a buying team of a regional hospital. This presentation was one of my largest target accounts. The current vendor was in a very favorable position. Their company had a solid product and delivered responsive service.

The incumbent sales rep had a personal relationship with the purchasing agent. The other companies competing for the business also had good products and services.

I knew that if we were to have a shot at this deal, we needed to flip the script. A week before the presentation, we asked the head nurse at their main facility if we could spend a day at the nursing station observing the flow of information.

During this day, we learned about the problems they faced related to the outcomes they desired. Essentially, the hospital wanted to fulfill its mission: "Deliver outstanding patient care." As we talked with nurses and observed the flow of information through the nursing station, we discovered the outcomes they desired as well as things that stood in the way.

When it came time for the presentation, we led with outcomes. We talked about how we could help the hospital fulfill its mission of "delivering outstanding patient care." We talked about the necessary outcomes at the nursing stations, which are the point of delivery for patient care.

Then, we gave specific examples of what we observed at the nursing station and how we would change it. At the end of the presentation, we showed a few slides about our company, our award-winning products, and a few references.

I am proud to say that we won the deal. It was a life-changing deal for me and the business. All of it happened because the presentation was delivered around outcomes instead of products.

Several years later, I was consulting the sales team of a German software company. Led by engineers, the company was proud of its product. The sales reps were coached to bring their laptop computers on each sales call. The goal was to demonstrate the software during the first meeting.

The software was impressive; to the average businessperson, the demonstration gave them two thoughts. First, they were impressed with the technical prowess of the company. Second, they wondered how this could help their business.

Noticing the disconnect, I recommended a new sales strategy. Reps brought only a notepad to the initial meeting. The conversation moved from talking about the product to talking about the prospect's desired outcomes.

The sales reps shared examples of how other companies with similar desired outcomes had achieved their goals. This simple shift from products to outcomes led to a dramatic increase in pipeline and close rate.

How can you change your presentations? What if you were not allowed to talk about your company and products until the second half of your presentation? What if you had to spend the first time talking about the buyers' goals and the outcomes you could deliver? I challenge you to try this and see what happens!

Proposals

Most proposals follow the same boring pattern as sales presentations. While a proposal does need to include information on your product and pricing, what if it began and ended with outcomes?

When it comes to delivering bad news, leadership trainers like to talk about a "feedback sandwich." You have probably been served a few of these over your career.

Instead of beginning with the bad news, you first share something you like about the person. Then you share the hard feedback. To end, you share something else you like about the person. While no one enjoys hard conversations, the feedback sandwich makes unpleasant news a little more palatable.

Your proposals can follow the feedback sandwich model. For me, the price page is bad news. After all, nobody likes to spend money. So, instead of leading with price, begin your proposal with outcomes. Here is how this could look:

1. Executive Summary

The first page outlines what you learned about their goals and the outcomes you can deliver.

2. Business Goals

List their business goals to show you understand what they want to accomplish.

3. Outcomes

Describe as many outcomes as you can deliver. Show a vision for a better future. Give a brief description of each one and how it will help the prospect achieve their goals.

4. Recommendation

Now, you can talk about the product and services. As you do this, connect the dots between the features of the product and the outcomes.

5. Investment - ROI

Zig Ziglar recommended that we do not use words like price. Use words like investment amount. Always show the outcomes with the investment amount on this page. When there are savings involved, show the return they will get on the investment. Under this, bullet out the most important outcomes.

6. Implementation Plan

The last page of a proposal should outline the steps for implementation. If you have done a good job understanding their needs and desired outcomes, you can feel comfortable assuming the deal is done. If objections come up, you can handle them. You will be pleasantly surprised at how this approach tends to reduce the number of objections.

Your proposals need to be able to stand on their own. In today's business environment with multiple decision-makers and influencers, this document may be the only thing that some of the buying team sees. Make sure that when they read it, they feel enlightened and inspired!

If you can keep these five words in your mind, "It is all about them," you will never go wrong. Focus on the outcomes they desire and the problems standing in the way. Take the dollar signs out of your eyes. When you do that, your message will resonate, and you will have more sales opportunities than ever before.

Important Points

1. Ask each person on your sales team to give you their elevator pitch. Does it focus on outcomes or product?

2. Listen in on your sales team's prospecting calls. Does the approach focus on outcomes or product?

3. Look at your sales collateral and proposals through the lens of your ideal client. What do you need to change?

Section 3: The Flywheels – Marketing & Sales Processes

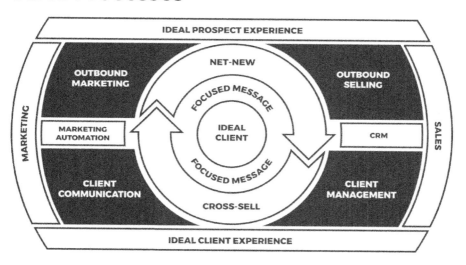

With the ideal client in mind, so far you have increased the force of your engine by enhancing ideal client experience. You have fueled your engine with a focused message. Now, we turn our attention to the flywheels: your marketing and sales processes.

Boil a business down to its most essential level and you will find two things: people and processes. The *Oxford Dictionary* defines process as: "A systematic series of mechanized or chemical operations that are performed in order to produce something." Your Revenue Growth Engine needs processes.

Walk through most departments of any company and you will find processes in action. Finance has processes for billing and collections. HR has processes for onboarding and firing. Logistics has processes for shipping and receiving. These processes ensure that these key business functions run smoothly.

Step into a marketing and sales department and what do you find? In my experience, it is less process-driven and more like the Wild West. Marketing runs some campaigns or hosts an event. Sales managers tell their reps to "go make some calls," or maybe they run a blitz. Most of these are one-time actions with very little planning or consistency.

What if you could put marketing and sales processes in place that run with the same productivity as your other business processes?

In this section, you will learn how to create marketing and sales processes for the two key drivers of business growth: net-new and cross-sell. The net-new processes are outbound marketing and outbound selling. Cross-sell processes are client management and client communication.

As you read, consider what cylinders of your net-new engine are in place and what aspects need to be built. For the cylinders that are in place, how could they be improved?

Chapter 8: Net-New Marketing Processes - Outbound Marketing

I used to like fishing. As a boy, I had a subscription to *Field & Stream* magazine. I would pore over each issue, looking for ways to attract more fish. My tackle box was filled with the latest crankbaits, spinner baits, and various colors of plastic worms. All of this was with the hope of maybe attracting a fish.

> Rather than fishing, businesses do better by farming and hunting.

The older I get, the less I like fishing. Sure, it can be relaxing to be outside on a sunny day, but the realities of fishing are that many days you don't catch anything. I don't like to wait for the fish to come to me. I want to go and get them.

I especially do not like the idea of fishing when it comes to business. To consistently grow revenue, you cannot just hope that an ideal prospect will happen to come by your website or call you. As they say, "Hope is not a strategy."

Darrell Amy

Rather than fishing, businesses do better by farming and hunting. By farming, I am planting and cultivating seeds that have a very good chance of turning into food. By hunting, I am actively tracking my prey. This combination is much more sustainable than fishing.

Interestingly, in the sales world, we talk about farmers and hunters. Much of today's marketing world seems to be more dedicated to fishing, hoping that some buyers will float by, nibble on our special offers, and create a lead. Unless you have a very large addressable market, this is not a sustainable business strategy.

Today, we hear a lot about inbound sales, the marketing equivalent of fishing. This strategy can work well if you need leads. It works in the B2C space when you have a large addressable market, such as selling swimming pools or roofing in a metro area with hundreds of thousands of homes. It can also work well for large B2B markets. In this case, you need leads with people who are actively buying, so inbound marketing works well.

Let me be clear on this point: if you have identified your ideal clients, you do not need leads. You already know who these companies and contacts are. What you need is engagement.

When you have already identified your ideal clients, the role of marketing shifts from fishing to farming and hunting. Don't get me wrong, it is nice when a lead comes in. However, there is too much at stake in the growth of your business just to hope for a lead to come in.

142

Unlike the individual consumer that is looking for an answer to a pressing problem like installing a new swimming pool or needing to fix a leaky roof, most B2B prospects do not understand their problems and the potential solutions. Thus, they are often not actively looking. By the time they are looking, it is often because a competitor has brought the problem to their attention and they are already engaged in a sales process.

In the B2B space, for every ideal prospect that is actively looking for what you provide, many more also need what you provide, but do not yet know it. In his book, *The New Solution Selling*, Keith Eades talks about two types of needs: felt needs and latent needs. Some of your prospects have felt needs. They know they have a problem and are actively looking for a solution. The vast majority of your prospects have latent needs. These are big problems, but your prospects are not aware of the impact.

So, what should you focus on before you invest in inbound marketing? Outbound marketing!

Outbound marketing is the process of initiating communication, actively listening, and purposefully engaging with ideal prospects.

With an outbound marketing strategy, you consistently share valuable information with key contacts in your ideal client accounts. Then, you listen to identify opportunities. As they begin to respond, you engage the sales team.

Let's explore the components of an outbound marketing program: Coverage Strategy, Messaging Cadence, and Response System.

Coverage Strategy

The goal of outbound marketing is 100 percent coverage: Every key decision-maker and influencer in your ideal prospect accounts hears from your business on a regular basis with valuable insights. You are consistently on their radar.

One of my favorite things to hear when I run into prospects is, "Wow, I see you everywhere. You're in my inbox, my mailbox, my social media, and even in the magazines I read." That always makes me smile; it means I am consistently on their radar.

Pulling off 100 percent coverage requires a process. Here are the three components of a coverage strategy.

1. Which Personas?

The first part of your coverage strategy is knowing which people you want to target in your ideal prospect accounts. As discussed earlier, research presented in *The Challenger Customer* revealed that there are an average of 6.8 decision-makers and influencers in the average B2B transaction. From a marketing perspective, this means that you have multiple entry points into an account. You also have multiple people to influence. The key is to identify the key roles in each account you want to target.

As you worked on your ideal client experience, you identified the core constituents involved in a sale. These are the contacts who need 100 percent coverage.

2. What Frequency?

The second part of your coverage strategy is frequency: How often do you want to get on their radar? Ultimately, you want to be a consistent resource to your ideal prospects.

You may be thinking, "That's great, but we can't email them every day." You are correct. Remember, your messaging cadence includes multiple media. In the next section, we will explore email, direct mail, and social media messaging. As well, we'll look at targeted advertising on websites and social media platforms.

You also need to remember that you are using a focused message on the outcomes desired by your ideal prospects. The more focused your message, the more your prospects will pay attention. If your message centers on your company and your products, you will get tuned out quickly, no matter what frequency you adopt.

For your outbound marketing program, I would recommend starting with the goal of getting on your ideal prospect's radar at least once a week. Remember, this involves email, but it should also include social media and advertising. Once a prospect begins to engage, then you can increase the frequency and personalization.

3. What Level of Customization?

The third decision for your coverage strategy is your level of customization: How much do you want to customize the message to individual companies? Your decision here requires you to balance efficiency with effectiveness.

The most efficient way is to focus on groups of buyer personas. Earlier, in the focused message section, we talked about identifying the roles of decision-makers and influencers in your ideal accounts. Each of these roles desires similar business outcomes. To maximize efficiency, you can create and send messages based on your knowledge of the outcomes that each buyer persona wants. For example, if you are targeting the chief executive, finance director, and I.T. manager in an account, then you could create messaging for each persona.

The most effective way is to customize communication to every single prospect. Based on what you know about the account and the specific issues they are facing, you can customize your messages for their specific business outcomes.

Send Relevant Messages

Once you've developed your coverage strategy, you are ready to engage. There are multiple ways you can communicate directly with your ideal prospects. In this section, we will discuss the most common ones.

However, as you build your message strategy, you need to remember your goal is to help ideal prospects by bringing their problems to the surface. You are turning latent needs into felt needs. How do you do this? You focus your message on the outcomes that your buyer personas desire. The more focused your messages, the better the results.

If you did a good job creating outcomes inventories for your ideal buyer personas you should have no problem coming up with focused messages. If you are struggling to come up with a relevant message, go back and review the chapter on creating a focused marketing message.

There are several outbound channels you can use along with two different ways to use these channels.

Email

The most common way to communicate with prospects is through email. Search for "email marketing stats" and you will discover that email remains an effective marketing strategy. One HubSpot study showed that 78 percent of marketers have seen increased engagement in email over the past 12 months.[x]

When sending emails, make sure to be aware of the government regulations in your area. You need systems in place to make sure that unsubscribe requests are honored. Carpet bombing lists of unverified, untargeted email addresses is spam. Most of these messages will never make it to the inbox. Sending focused messages with relevant information to verified emails is vastly different.

Social Media Inboxes

Direct messaging should not stop at email. Some prospects may never open your email because it has been trapped in a spam filter. This is where social media inboxes come in. LinkedIn allows you to send direct messages through InMail to prospects. Based on your subscription level, LinkedIn limits the number of messages you can send to people who are not first-degree connections, so you do not want to overuse this tactic. However, the LinkedIn inbox can be a powerful way to reach targeted accounts.

Right now, you may be wondering if the marketer should be involved in sending messages down to the individual account and contact level. With your ideal prospects, the answer is, "Yes." The goal is 100 percent coverage. If you cannot get through with email, then use alternative methods.

Direct Mail

Direct mail provides another layer of communication. While sending a letter or postcard may sound old-school, the reality is that people still check their mail. According to the Data and Marketing Association, 42.2 percent of recipients either scan or read the direct mail they get. This should get your attention.

Social Media

Another way to get on the radar of your ideal prospects is through social media. A quick Google search for social media statistics reveals that most B2B decision-makers are using LinkedIn along with other social media channels.

By becoming active on social media as a company, two things will happen. First, you will get impressions as your focused message shows up in your ideal prospects' social media feeds. Second, you create opportunities for engagement as people like, comment, and share your posts. These provide opportunities for responding, which we will explore later in this chapter.

Develop a regular social cadence for your company. Be present on social media channels at least once a day. Make sure not to skip the weekends, as this is when many executives review and plan their weeks.

Whenever you can, tag your ideal prospects in your social media posts. For example, if your ideal prospect is a healthcare clinic group and you see in the news that they have opened a new location, share the news article and tag them in the post. You could create a post on your company's social media page like this: "Congratulations to **ABC Healthcare** and CEO Mary Smith for continuing to expand services to our community." This will get you on the radar of the CEO and other people in the company.

Targeted Advertising

A less direct way to get on the radar of your prospects is through targeted advertising. In the old days, advertising meant broadcasting your message across TV, radio, and billboards. With an ideal client strategy, you want to narrowcast your advertising, focusing on the people inside your targeted accounts.

149

New online advertising platforms allow you to target ads to specific companies and people. These ads show up as they are surfing the Internet and scrolling through social media feeds.

There are several ways to serve up online ads. The simplest way is through retargeting advertising. Even the best websites only convert a tiny percentage of visitors to leads. Retargeting lets you serve up ads to people who have visited your website. Over the coming weeks or months, you can serve up display ads that appear when they visit websites or use mobile apps that show ads. These retargeted ads can be segmented. For example, if your website visitor clicked on a landing page promoting your next webinar, you might serve up ads reminding them about it. The most popular retargeting platform is Google. However, LinkedIn also offers retargeting, allowing you to serve up ads to your previous web visitors.

The second way is account-based advertising. This lets you target your ads to people inside companies on your ideal prospect list. The way this works is fairly simple. Most companies have a dedicated IP address for their network. Companies like DemandBase and Terminus let you upload your target list and create ads. These ads are served to people inside your target accounts.

The third way to advertise is through social media. LinkedIn Matched Audiences allows you to create audiences based on specific accounts or contacts you want to target. Basically, you upload your ideal prospect list to LinkedIn, set up your ads, and you're up and running. If you want to slightly broaden your reach rather than identify specific accounts, you can use criteria such as the company size and industry to create your audience. With this strategy, you can reach your target audience.

Advertising on social media platforms includes banner ads. You can also sponsor posts, paying to have your updates featured directly in a social media feed.

Similar to direct messaging, all of your ads need to include a very focused message. Remember, buyers do not buy products, they buy outcomes. Therefore, you must focus your headlines around the outcomes your ideal clients want to achieve.

What is a win when it comes to direct messaging? While you certainly want a response, the reality is that impressions are also wins. Not every message will get a response from every target. However, most messages will get an impression. If your messages are focused on the outcomes your ideal clients desire, then that impression will be a good one.

When it comes to reaching your ideal client, use a multi-channel approach. Develop a quarterly cadence of communication. Your cadence might include weekly emails and a monthly direct mail campaign. For clients that are not responsive to email, try a quarterly LinkedIn message. Remember, you are trying to get on their radar.

Listen and Engage

It's amazing what happens when you listen. Later, in the outbound sales chapter, we will recommend that each salesperson listens to their target accounts. However, marketing should also be about listening.

151

The goal of your listening process is to discover two things: triggers and insights.

Triggers. Since you know who your target clients are, you can watch for specific events that indicate they might be open to engaging with your company. This could include new product launches, new locations, or new investments. Most importantly, by listening, you begin to understand what is happening in these ideal accounts. Then you can tailor your communication to their needs.

Insights. Marketing is responsible for creating messaging. Whether you are writing content for your website, creating a whitepaper, drafting a blog article, or writing a social media post, you need to share insights that are relevant to your target market. By listening, you get insight into the challenges and outcomes your ideal prospects want. Without this, your messaging is going to be bland and much less effective.

Where to Listen

These days, there are many places to get insights. Some sources like social media, company blogs, and news are free, only requiring your time and effort. Other sources like data and intent services require a budget but are worth the investment for many companies.

Your Website

On any given day, hundreds of people may be visiting your website. Some are current clients; others are visitors from around the world. When an ideal prospect visits your website, you need to know.

Most marketing automation platforms will tell you what companies are coming to your website. Once a contact at your ideal prospect has interreacted with your messaging by clicking a link in an email or completing a form on your website, your marketing automation software may be able to identify when they come back to your site.

Lead scoring is a feature of most marketing automation platforms that lets you assign points for every action a website visitor takes, such as visiting a page or filling out a form. The idea is that when a visitor accumulates enough points, it flags the marketer. This is fine for average prospects. When it comes to your ideal prospects, though, you want to be notified. Configure your marketing automation platform to notify you when an ideal prospect hits your website.

Social Media

The first place to listen is on social media. Start by following all of the ideal prospect companies and key contacts on social media. Since you're gathering intel, I recommend that you look at the platforms your ideal clients are using. Currently, most businesses are active on LinkedIn, Twitter, and Facebook. Your specific industry may use different platforms.

First, follow every one of your ideal prospect accounts. On LinkedIn and Twitter, you search for the company and click "Follow." On Facebook, you find their Facebook page and "Like" it.

Next, set up social media listening dashboards. The reason you need to do this is that your social media feeds will become clogged with irrelevant information from non-target accounts, not to mention friends and celebrities! You can set up a listening dashboard in each of the platforms. LinkedIn's Sales Navigator lets you tag and organize accounts. Twitter lets you create lists, allowing you to make a list of your ideal clients.

You can also find third-party social media listening platforms that allow you to put all of your social media feeds into one place. This feature is also a part of some marketing automation platforms.

Company Blogs

Your ideal clients continually release news and articles. You can follow their blogs using their RSS (Real Simple Syndication) feeds. There are many great RSS readers that allow you to follow blogs and news from multiple companies. These include products like Feedly and Flipboard.

When you see an interesting blog that might be relevant to other ideal prospects and clients, share it on your company's social media pages. This will help you get on their radar, generate goodwill from the exposure, and demonstrate that you are paying attention to what they are saying to the market.

Business News

Follow local business journals in the markets you serve. If you target a specific industry, pay attention to their industry news sources. As most of these sources have both social media and RSS feeds, you can follow them there.

Similar to company blogs, share interesting business news on your social media pages. Congratulate companies for growing, opening new locations, or launching new products.

Search

The next place to listen is in search engines. You can configure Google to look for specific keywords related to your target accounts. When you set this up, you can have it trigger an email to you when news is released.

Data Subscriptions

Companies like Dun & Bradstreet and Zoom Info offer subscription services that allow you to monitor current news and insights on your current accounts. While most companies use these services for finding contacts, they can also be used to find insights.

Set up your data service with triggers that notify you when specific things happen. The first trigger you should set up will be based on your ideal client profile. You can have the data platform notify you when a new company meets the criteria of your ideal client.

There are many other triggers you can configure. For example, you might want to be notified when any of your target accounts open a new location. You might want a trigger when they raise additional capital. You can also be notified when new key contacts are added.

Intent Data

Imagine if you could know when people in your ideal prospect companies are searching for the products you sell? There is a growing category of companies measuring buyer intent. Simply put, they look at search queries coming from specific company IP addresses. Based on this data, they can tell you what companies are actively searching for the products you sell.

Currently, most of these services are targeted at the enterprise level, requiring enterprise-level budgets. I expect that, over time, these services will be more attainable for the mid-market.

Process

With your listening system in place, now it's time to listen! Marketers should block out a significant amount of time each day for this process. I recommend that this be one of the first things you do each morning. Listening sets you up for a successful day because it keeps your finger on the pulse of your ideal clients. You will get fresh ideas. You will also discover actionable insights that can be used in real-time to engage accounts through messaging or to hand off to the sales team.

Create a daily checklist that includes every source you want to monitor. You can make this even easier by configuring your web browser to automatically open up all of your listening tabs. With all of your social media, data, and other sources open, you can work your way across the tabs looking for actionable insights.

Know what you are looking for. Remember, you want to find insights and triggers. Scan through the social media feeds, news headlines, and data sources with an eye open for insights or triggers. Always be asking two questions:

1. Insight: What can I learn?

2. Triggers: What can I act on?

As you listen, make sure to document what you learn. Copy and paste relevant information about an ideal account or contact into your CRM. Share that information with the sales rep for that account. Then, create an email or text with a link to the source.

Engaging

Intel is great, but it is meaningless if you do not do something with it. You need to respond to signals, engaging with ideal prospects.

With traditional inbound marketing, you are looking for a lead. This implies that the person on the other end is an active buyer, waiting with bated breath for a salesperson to call so they can sign on the dotted line. In the B2B world with multiple decision-makers, this is a fantasy that rarely happens. As a result, you hear the salespeople complaining about the quality of the leads.

With outbound marketing to ideal prospects, instead of leads, salespeople need an "in." They need a reason to engage and deepen a relationship with a decision-maker or influencer.

This shift in mindset from leads to engagement is critical. From a marketing perspective, it redefines success from leads to setting the table for sales to have a conversation. From a sales perspective, it changes the level of expectation for what comes over from marketing.

Many marketing teams are so focused on creating leads that they neglect to listen and respond to the signals coming in. Here are some suggestions on how you can respond: engage directly, update your CRM, and hand off to sales.

Engage Directly

Most of today's marketing depends on autoresponders. Canned messages are okay when it comes to your average accounts, but when an ideal client comes across your radar, it makes much more sense to give this your personal attention.

Responding does not have to be complicated; simply offer to help. Your job is not to try to sell anything. The goal is to set up a conversation with a sales rep.

So, when an ideal prospect engages with your emails, website, or social media, send a message offering your assistance. Here are some examples of how you could engage:

Email: "Hi! Thanks for responding to the email we sent last week. I hope you found the information helpful. I'd be happy to connect you with one of our account representatives to share how other local companies are navigating this challenge."

Twitter: "Hi! Thanks for engaging with our Twitter account. We really appreciate the re-tweet of the article about cyber security and compliance. I'm curious, what part of the article caught your attention?"

Chat: "Hi! Thanks for stopping by. We have a special report that goes deeper on the topics in our blog. Would you like me to send it to you?"

Website Visitor Data: "Hi! I noticed that you've been reading content on our website recently about our new virtual CFO service. We've helped a lot of local companies evaluate their options. I'd be happy to connect you with one of our representatives to talk about your challenges."

LinkedIn: "Thanks for your comments on the LinkedIn article we shared about creative ways to manage expenses. I hope you found the ideas helpful. Here's a link to a special report we wrote that you might also enjoy."

Facebook: "Hi! I wanted to reach out and say we really appreciated your sharing of our Facebook post about the local non-profit. We believe in helping our community. Thanks for being a bright light in our city."

You can engage on the appropriate channel. There are no rules here. Sometimes, it makes sense to send an email; other times, you can message through a social media platform. You might want to simply drop a thank you card in the mail. You may even want to send a gift along with some helpful material.

Not every interaction needs to begin with a direct call of an appointment with a rep. Engage them in digital conversation. Remember, these are your ideal prospects. Every one of them could be worth hundreds of thousands if not millions of dollars to your company. It's appropriate to treat them in a special way.

Should you engage based on data collected from your website? Years ago, reaching out to someone who was on your webpage seemed creepy. These days, everyone knows that companies are watching their interactions on their site. It's kind of like walking into a store. The people in the store know you are there. You do not think it strange when they say "Hi" or ask if they can help. Similarly, you should feel comfortable reaching out to ideal clients who are engaging with your emails, social media, or website.

Update Your CRM

Companies always complain about salespeople not updating their CRM. As an outbound marketing person, you should set the example by adding notes to the CRM. When you engage with an ideal prospect, make sure to copy the details of the intel you found, along with the details of the conversation.

Hand Off to Sales

Facilitate a smooth transition to the sales rep. If the ideal prospect says they would like to learn more, then introduce the rep. The easiest way to do this is by email. Simply create an informal email that introduces the rep to the prospect.

In addition to the introductory email, send a second message to the sales rep detailing the interaction thus far, so that the rep has context to pick up the conversation.

Companies should train their salespeople on how to handle these types of opportunities. With ideal prospects, most of these are traditional sales leads where the buyer has a felt need and urgency to buy. That will happen sometimes, but most of the time, these are an opportunity for a rep to get a foot in the door and begin a relationship. These interactions give the reps the opportunity to begin a relationship of trust with an ideal prospect. Over time, they can work to turn latent needs into felt needs.

Outbound marketing requires a coverage plan, consistent messaging, and intentional listening to engage. As you do this, you will become a "regular" with your ideal prospects. As long as you make sure to focus your message on their needs, they will expect to see you. In time, you will earn their trust and, eventually, their business.

Important Points

1. Rather than fishing, businesses do better by farming and hunting.

2. The goal of outbound marketing is 100 percent coverage: Every key decision-maker and influencer in your ideal prospect accounts hears from your business on a regular basis with valuable insights. You are consistently on their radar.

3. You are turning latent needs into felt needs. How do you do this? You focus your message on the outcomes that your buyer personas desire. The more focused your messages, the better the results.

4. The goal of your listening process is to discover two things: triggers and insights.

5. Listening sets you up for a successful day because it keeps your finger on the pulse of your ideal clients. You will get fresh ideas. You will also discover actionable insights that can be used in real-time to engage accounts through messaging or to hand off to the sales team.

6. Intel is great, but it is meaningless if you do not do something with it. You need to respond to signals, engaging with ideal prospects.

Chapter 9: Net-New Sales Processes - Outbound Selling

T he job of salespeople is to bring latent needs to the surface to create felt needs. These become sales opportunities. This is where I think most sales reps have it backwards. They spend most of their time looking for a hot opportunity with the buyer who is active in the buying cycle rather than working to build relationships of trust where they can turn latent needs into felt needs. If 1 in 100 prospects is currently "in the market," many sales reps will spend their days trying to find that one person, totally ignoring the 99 other businesses.

> In the sales world, there is a constant discussion about whether salespeople are hunters or farmers.

In the sales world, there is a constant discussion about whether salespeople are hunters or farmers. The hunter camp says that reps should focus on taking down hot deals. The farmer camp says that reps should take a more long-term approach, developing relationships with prospects and clients. The reality is somewhere in the middle. A solid outbound selling strategy accomplishes two things: it feeds the hunter, finding the people in the market with felt needs while farming the larger market with insights that position the rep for future success.

"First-in wins," was a phrase commonly heard in the bullpen at my first B2B sales job. Prospecting for business in a way that turns latent needs into felt needs allows reps to get in the deal early. Since they create the deal, they participate in defining the parameters, and the closing percentages and profits become higher.

The challenge is that most sales teams struggle to prospect consistently. The moment that a sales rep gets comfortable and complacent with their current results, prospecting goes out the door.

Prospecting needs to be effective, efficient, and measurable. Effective prospecting happens when reps know what to say and how to handle the brush offs and objections confidently. It also happens when reps know exactly whom to call, rather than fumbling through CRM records, spreadsheets, and lists. Measurable prospecting is enabled by systems that automatically track outbound prospecting activity rather than hoping reps will report their calls.

Sadly, most prospecting is not accurately measured. While companies meticulously measure and analyze inbound marketing data, sales activity data gets ignored. This is inexcusable, since prospecting is a leading indicator of net-new sales results. We all know the saying, "You cannot manage what you cannot measure." If you want to manage the net-new business, you need to be able to measure prospecting activity.

Your outbound selling system needs to be running smoothly. In this chapter, you will see a framework to help you identify target accounts, prospect with sequences, and nurture the funnel.

With the right processes in place, prospecting can be highly effective and possible. Furthermore, the systems used to prospect can also be used to influence buying teams. This becomes critical in a world where decisions are rarely made by one person.

In this chapter, we'll explore the three cylinders of outbound selling related to growing net-new business:

1. Target Accounts

2. Prospecting System

3. Influencing Buying Teams

With these three cylinders running at peak performance, not only will you find more ideal prospects, you'll also increase your close rate. All of this will help you drive more net-new business.

Target Accounts

Earlier we talked about your ideal client and how to craft a clear message that resonates with them. Now it is time to find the target accounts that meet this profile.

This begins by identifying the rough characteristics of your target accounts. One business I was recently working with discovered that their ideal client was a business with 25-250 knowledge workers. We discovered that they were strong in some vertical markets like legal, healthcare, and education. Furthermore, they preferred to work with companies that had local decision-making authority.

Armed with this profile, we began searching through databases. There are many good sources of target data like Dun & Bradstreet Hoovers or Zoom Info. Choose a source that fits your needs and budget.

Begin your search by narrowing down the geography. In the south Florida area, we discovered that there were roughly 90,000 businesses!

This is a good time to pause. This company had six people on their sales team. When it came to prospecting, the basic instruction was to, "Go make some calls." 90,000 business establishments split between six reps meant that each rep had 15,000 accounts to call on. If a sales rep made 30 calls a day, it would take 500 days or 2 business years to make just one call on each account. No wonder they were frustrated. Simply focusing these salespeople on the right target accounts could transform the team.

Next, we began to filter the results, choosing companies with 25-250 employees. This narrowed the field considerably. Then, we began selecting industries with knowledge workers where the company had previous success. Finally, we chose companies that were headquartered in the local area.

By the time these filters were applied there were about 1,800 target accounts. That meant each rep had 300 target accounts on which to focus.

This company also worked with multiple decision-makers, usually at the finance, technology, and head executive level. Now it was clear that they needed the data on CEO/President, CIO/VP Finance, and CIO/VP Technology/IT Manager for each of these target accounts. Once acquired, this data was loaded into the CRM, clearly marked as a target account, and assigned to a sales rep.

Before we proceed, let me offer some advice on acquiring data. First of all, purchased data will never be perfect or complete. You'll never get all the contacts for each company. However, you need a baseline to get started.

> With the Target Accounts clearly identified, now you can craft sales expectations.

Second, data is always shifting. New ideal target accounts are moving into your area or starting up. Other companies are moving out or going bankrupt. I recommend you find a data partner that can monitor your target account profile and let you know when new ones move in.

With the Target Accounts clearly identified, now you can craft sales expectations. The high-level goal should be that every one of the key contacts in these Target Accounts knows who your company is, regularly hearing from your sales team with useful information that could help them improve their business.

With the south Florida company, the message from leadership was clear: You are free to call on any of the 90,000 businesses in your target area. However, you absolutely, 100% must call on the 300 Target Accounts that have been assigned to you. If not, we will assign them to someone else who will call on them.

On a more practical level, your Target Account program needs to have some activity expectations. With our example company, they wanted their sales reps to contact the three decision-makers in each target account at least twice a year. (We'll explore how you can do this in the next section.) They also wanted their sales team to follow these decision-makers on social media so they could stay updated on useful news and opportunities.

All this needs to be documented in your Target Account playbook. Write down the description of your Target Account. Clearly explain your goal for these accounts. Then, document the activity expectations.

Next, you need to develop a prospecting strategy.

Prospecting

One touch simply does not cut it in today's world. Salesforce.com research found that it takes six to eight touches with a prospect to get an appointment.[xi] Sirius Decisions' took this even further, discovering that it takes eight to twelve attempts to reach a decision-maker by phone--even when they are interested in your products or solutions![xii]

> Salespeople need to inspire both trust and attention. These are earned by consistently reaching out with ideas that prospects see as helpful in achieving their outcomes.

Whatever the number, the point is simple: you must reach out to prospects multiple times if you expect to get results.

Salespeople need to inspire both trust and attention. These are earned by consistently reaching out with ideas that prospects see as helpful in achieving their outcomes. As trust is earned, appointments happen.

Unfortunately, many sales reps are "one-and-done" when it comes to prospecting. They make a call or send an email, hoping to find a hot opportunity. When they do not get through, they then put a note to reach out again in another ninety days.

Today's sales rep is blessed with many ways to communicate with prospects, including the phone, email, direct mail, and a variety of social media channels. While these multiple channels create opportunities, they can also feel overwhelming.

Every prospector knows the law of ratios. Only a small percentage of dials will get through. SPAM filters combined with the sheer volume of email most people get means only a handful of emails you send get read. Direct mail is similar, with only a small percentage of items getting more than a glance. Social media posts only get seen by the small percentage of your audience that happens to be scrolling when you post.

Smart prospectors realize that getting in touch with the most prospects requires flexibility to communicate over multiple channels. Look at it this way. Let's say you only get a one percent appointment ratio on the following four communication channels: phone, email, direct mail, and LinkedIn. If you add all these together, building a multi-channel prospecting strategy, you could get a 4X bump in your results.

In today's environment, the formula for prospecting success is as follows: Reach out to prospects with ideas that matter. Do this consistently across multiple communication channels.

Fortunately, there is a new technology that makes this possible. I call these sales sequences.

What Is a Sales Sequence?

A sales sequence is a planned series of prospecting touches using multiple channels over a period of time. For example, a sequence might flow as follows:

Day 1: Email

Day 2: Phone Call

Day 2: Direct Mail Letter

Day 3: Social Touch on LinkedIn

Day 7: Email

Day 8: Phone Call

Day 9: Direct Mail Card

Day 10: Social Touch

Day 13: Email

Day 14: Social Media Message

Over a two-week period, this prospect would have heard from you up to fourteen times. Remember, however, that not all messages will be seen. So, while fourteen times may sound excessive, it takes a lot of touches to get through.

Imagine how much you will increase the odds of getting through to your target accounts when you use a multi-touch, multi-channel sequence.

Sales Sequence Technology

While all of this sounds good in theory, as a recovering sales rep myself, I know that salespeople tend to struggle with managing lots of details. Fortunately, there is an emerging class of sales enablement software that automates the process of launching and following up on sequences.

HGTV ran a show called Semi-Homemade. This show taught you how to combine canned food with a few of your own ingredients to quickly create homemade dishes.

Sequences allow reps to do the same thing. Just like nobody wants to eat canned food, no prospect wants a canned email. With sequence software, reps can quickly add their own flair to pre-written sequences of emails, call-backs, and social touches. Reps can consider what they know about the prospect from previous interactions or referrals. They can also do a quick search on Google and social media to find areas to add insight.

In just a few minutes, they can launch a series of touches to a prospect. While it takes a small amount of effort to launch a sequence, the true gain in efficiency happens in the follow up. Phone prospecting blocks become hyper-efficient. Instead of sitting down and wondering whom to call, reps open their sequence software to find pre-populated lists of phone calls. As you build the sequences, you can include talking points, call scripts, and voicemail scripts. Now salespeople do not have to wonder whom to call or what to say.

This technology can create massive boosts in prospecting productivity. I have seen reps go from making under ten calls an hour to upwards of forty or more calls. This frees up massive amounts of time.

These sequences can also build social touch lists. These are promptings for the reps to reach out and touch the prospect on social media. There are many ways to do this. The key is to get on the prospect's radar.

One of the overlooked benefits of using social media as a prospecting tool is email notifications. Many people have their social media pages set to email them when someone likes, comments on, or re-shares their posts. The target that ignores your prospecting email may receive an email from Twitter and wonder who that person was who re-shared their tweet. By creating task lists of social touches, sequence software can prompt your reps to reach out and touch prospects at the right time during the prospecting sequence.

The Message

Whether you leverage sequence technology or not, your prospecting activity needs to be backed with a relevant message. In research for the book *Insight Selling,* Mike Schultz and John Doerr studied more than 700 business-to-business purchases made by buyers who represent $3.1 billion in annual purchasing power. They discovered that buyers want salespeople to bring them insights. "Today's sales winners harness the power of ideas."

The implications of prospecting are simple. If you want to get attention with a buyer, bring them ideas that can help them achieve the outcomes they want. Earlier in this book, we talked about the reality that buyers do not buy products; they buy outcomes. Therefore, your prospecting material must lead with outcomes.

Buyers do not care about your salespeople. They do not care that they are "new in the area," or that they "just want to stop by." However, in the absence of enabling salespeople with genuine insights to share that can help buyers achieve their outcomes, this is the ineffective garbage that reps fall back on.

Working on outcomes is like sharpening your saw. In *The Seven Habits of Highly Effective People*, Stephen Covey tells the story of two lumberjacks. One worked relentlessly to cut down trees. The other stopped and took breaks throughout the day to sharpen their saw. The first lumberjack thought the second one was lazy and unmotivated. It turned out that the second one outperformed the first because he was working with a sharp saw.

Working on your message is the sales equivalent of sharpening your saw. If you skipped the section on presenting a clear message, there is a good chance your saw is dull. I encourage you to go back and do this. Interview clients and write success stories. Build an outcomes inventory. Use this as the basis for every prospecting email, phone script, and social touch. Talk about outcomes in every sales meeting. Educate and create a culture of insight in your sales team.

Sample Scripts

Outcomes drive your prospecting message. For example, if you sell project management software to construction companies, you might learn that the outcomes they want are faster job completion and better terms with subcontractors. Lead your messages with these outcomes, like this:

For a phone script:
"This is Darrell with Construction Cloud. I am calling to set an appointment because we help contractors complete their jobs faster and get better terms with subcontractors."

For an email:

Subject: Complete Jobs Faster

Body: I have ideas that other construction companies have used to complete jobs faster while also enabling them to get better terms with their suppliers.

To help, we prepared an eBook titled, "Three Ways to Complete Jobs Ahead of Schedule." You can download it here at: www.constructioncloudexample.com/book

To your success,

Darrell Amy

For social media:

Share your company's blog articles with strategies to complete jobs faster and improve sub-contractor terms. Follow your prospects and comment on their posts with relevant insights as the opportunity arises.

Sharing relevant outcomes is key to effective prospecting. The more you can integrate outcomes into your message, the more results you will see from your prospecting efforts.

Measuring Success

I will never forget one of my early experiences as a new sales rep. Our job included hard-core door-to-door prospecting to local businesses. I was sent to spend the day riding with a tenured rep to watch and learn from him. After spending most of the morning babysitting current customers, we found ourselves enjoying a pizza buffet for lunch. As we were settling our bill, there was a fishbowl full of business cards. I am sure the restaurant intended to give away a free buffet in exchange for some contact information. The sales rep I was riding with had different intentions. When the cashier was not looking, he stuck his hand in the fishbowl and grabbed a wad of cards.

Back in the car, he looked at me, smiled, and said, "Prospecting!" Later that day, when it came time to turn in his call report, he counted the cards, wrote down the number, and turned in the call sheet.

Later, as I became a sales manager, that experience haunted me. I knew that the leading indicator of pipeline health was prospecting. However, I had no accurate way to measure prospecting activity. While I required reps to turn in activity reports, I knew that most of the data was, at best, an exaggeration.

Sequences give you a way to measure prospecting accurately. These platforms track the number of sequences launched and tasks completed (calls, social touches). You can see this in real time, letting you know if your sales team is filling the funnel or fudging the data.

Every sales team will track activity metrics slightly differently. Here are a few high-level data points to consider:

Sequences Launched

Set a target for sequences launched per day or week. If you have a sales model that includes door-to-door field prospecting, set the expectation that the call does not count until the sequence is launched. The good news is that if you have been begging your field sales reps to enter data into the CRM, your sequence platform should sync with your CRM. That will allow you to not only launch the sequence, but to update your database as well. You know that once a sequence is launched, at least your prospects will be getting emails. In addition to those emails, sequences set the stage for measurable phone prospecting.

Calls Made

Sequence software also lets you measure phone calls. When reps sit down to make phone calls during prospecting time blocks, they see a list of all the calls that need to be made. As they work through the list, each call is logged. There is no hiding. It is all measurable.

Social Touches

If you take my recommendation to use social media in your sequences, you can create a social touch task list. As salespeople click "complete" after reaching out to a prospect on social media, you can now measure their social media prospecting activity.

All of this should roll up into real-time dashboards. Sales leadership should never wonder how much activity is being completed. The leading indicators of prospecting are completely visible.

I recommend that you enable your reps to prospect efficiently, effectively, and measurably with sequence software. Give them sequences with content that focuses on the outcomes your prospects want. As you do, you will create both activity and accountability in the Net-New Sales quadrant of your Revenue Growth Engine.

Influence the Buying Team

Prospecting does not stop once you get the appointment. Very few sales involve one decision-maker. It makes sense when you realize that most businesses have a financial, operational, and technical aspect.

Salespeople face tremendous challenges with buying teams. Though they probably got in the door through one person, they now face the challenge of identifying the other members of the buying team, and then building credibility with each of them. Of course, each of these people has different priorities based on their roles.

While the rep's first-in contact may be excited, typically, other decision-makers and influencers are less than enthusiastic. To make matters worse, even if a rep is lucky enough to identify all the players, they may not get to meet with them face-to-face.

All of this creates friction in the buying process. You can remove some of the friction by providing your sales team with tools to help reduce it.

Decision-Maker's Survival Kit

Your "Decision-Maker's Survival Kit" provides helpful insights aimed at each member of the buying team.

The first thing you need from members of the buying team is trust. You can earn trust by showing *competency* and *credibility*.

Regarding competency, the buyer is thinking, "Do you understand my world and the outcomes I want to achieve?" There are many ways you can demonstrate this. Blog articles can address the common questions key decision-makers have during the buying process. Special reports or e-books could demonstrate the outcomes you can deliver that would be beneficial to various members of a buying team. These assets could be placed as calls-to-action on your website so that you can identify these people when they download the information.

> Regarding competency, the buyer is thinking, "Do you understand my world and the outcomes I want to achieve?"

In addition to competency, you need to establish credibility. The best way to do this is through success stories. As you create real-world case studies of your clients, consider segmenting them by the different types of buyers. For example, if your typical buying team includes the HR Director, CFO, and IT Manager, interview each of these people in your current account base. Write the success stories from their perspectives and use them to build credibility in the sales process. In addition to success stories, gather references from these positions and create reference sheets for each of your buyer-types.

You might consider creating a section of your website with resource pages that present this information. With marketing automation software running in the background, you can get insight as to how each buyer interacts with the content, signaling what their interests might be.

You could also create a physical "decision-maker's survival kit," where you bundle together information that is helpful to each type of decision-maker. Package it up professionally with some of your swag and some gift cards for a cup of coffee. Not only will this be helpful to the buying team, but it will also create a positive impression, building a competitive advantage.

Social Media Networking

Social media networking becomes a powerful tool for salespeople during the buying cycle. As the company works to demonstrate competency and credibility with the members of the buying team, sales reps can leverage social media to show their competency and credibility as well.

Skeptical buying team members that have been brought into the buying process go online to see if the sales rep knows what they are talking about. When they type the rep's name into Google or LinkedIn, the information they find can have a huge impact on how that decision-maker feels about doing any future business with that rep.

Sales reps need to have LinkedIn profiles that position them as both competent and credible. The headline and summary can reference outcomes that the rep delivers, along with why they are passionate about what they do. Buyer resources can be shared on the profile. Regular status updates can include useful information from the company's blog. References from current clients build credibility.

Larry Levine, the author of *Selling From the Heart,* coaches sales teams to integrate social media into the buying process. Experience has shown him that salespeople need to, "Get valuable before they get visible." This means that reps need to invest the time to have the right profile and content ready on the appropriate social media platforms. Then, they can leverage this to help win over buying teams.

Your salespeople should choose social media channels based on where your prospects live. In the B2B space, LinkedIn has become the de facto place for reps to build their online presence. However, many prospects are also active on social media platforms like Twitter, Instagram, and Facebook. Depending on your audience, you can determine how you want to leverage these platforms.

With a solid presence in place, reps can now leverage social media to connect and drive conversations with members of the buying team. The relationship with the primary buyer gives a great reason to send a custom message requesting a connection. ("I am working with Bob on some new ideas and would love to connect…") While reps may not be able to have face-to-face meetings with every influencer, they can certainly drive conversation online by sharing useful information through the messenger functions on the social media platform. Of course, savvy reps will also look at each buyer's social media profile to find areas of commonality such as where they went to school, their areas of interest, or non-profits they support.

Sequences are a key component in building a successful Revenue Growth Engine. It is the oil that lubricates everything and allows the engine to run at peak performance. Think of what happens to your engine when the oil runs dry? The engine stops, and so does income growth in a company without sequences. You will be amazed at the increase in revenue when your engine is running smoothly!

Important Points

1. A solid outbound selling strategy accomplishes two things: it feeds the hunter, finding the people in the market with felt needs while farming the larger market with insights that position the rep for future success.

2. Now it is time to find the target accounts that meet this profile. This begins by identifying the rough characteristics of your target accounts.

3. Influence Buying Teams.

4. Create content and case studies for each type of decision-maker and influencer.

5. Develop a Decision-Maker's Survival Kit.

6. Ensure your sales reps have social media profiles that make them look competent and credible.

Darrell Amy

Chapter 10: Cross-Sell Sales Processes - Client Management Part 1

O ver the years, I have seen a consistent trend in responses to client surveys: the only time they hear from the company is when something breaks, or it is time to renew the contract. In most cases, clients feel like the sales team is very interested in them until the deal closes. Once the product is delivered, they never hear from them again.

Most companies spend considerable time thinking about the pre-sales experience. In the quest for net-new business, it can be easy to overlook the experience after the sale. Doing this, however, overlooks a huge opportunity.

Sales professionals have a tremendous opportunity to cross-sell additional products and services to their clients. The revenue growth impact of being intentional about this can be astounding. All it takes is the tools and processes to enable excellent client management.

In the next two chapters, we will look at how you can enable your sales team during the three phases of the client experience: onboarding, during the relationship, and before upgrades.

Onboarding Experience

My first sales manager used to always ask us this question: "When is the best time to close a sale?" The correct answer was, "When you just sold something." I found this to be true over and over again. As a sales rep, when I had closed a sale, I had the Midas touch that seemed to turn the other things in my sales funnel into gold.

What if the best time to sell something to your new client was after they purchased from you? Think about it. They have already said "Yes" to your company. They are excited about the benefits they will be receiving.

Reaching out to your clients after they have purchased your product sets the stage for cross-selling. By focusing on the client experience after they sign the order, you open up new potential to grow your business. While they may not pull out their wallet right away, if you create a great onboarding experience, you set the table for additional sales during your relationship. If you provide a poor onboarding experience, you greatly reduce your chance of additional business.

Combatting buyer's remorse creates another compelling reason to develop a great onboarding experience. We have all experienced regret after saying "Yes" to a deal. We wonder if we made a good decision. We feel like we may have spent too much money. We worry about what happens if the company doesn't deliver what was promised. We are concerned about how our co-workers will like the change.

> Many companies make promises during the sales process, but when it comes to delivery, clients end up being underwhelmed and even angry.

In truth, the sale is only halfway complete when the prospect approves the deal. Think about the purchases you have made. You bought it because you anticipated the benefits that would come your way. However, even though you said "Yes," you still wonder if the company will deliver what they said they would.

Many companies make promises during the sales process, but when it comes to delivery, clients end up being underwhelmed and even angry. In light of their frustrations, they may even forget the reasons they bought the product in the first place.

At this point, they may try to cancel their order. Even if it doesn't go that far, they may feel a low-level resentment toward your company, which will hurt your relationship going forward. This is not what you are aiming for!

Instead, you want to replace buyer's remorse with buyer's delight. You want to create raving fans that love your company. You want clients that feel like you delivered everything you said you would—and more. You want clients that gladly give you referrals.

To make this happen, you need to create a memorable onboarding experience. You want a predictable process that reinforces why they bought from you and maximizes the chances that your clients will become enthusiastic fans. Let's look at each step carefully.

1. Find Creative Ways to Say Thank You

Chick-fil-A has had great success in the fast food industry as their stores generate more revenue than their next three competitors combined. How do they do this? They find as many ways as possible to say "Thank you" to their customers.

Sadly, saying these two small words is one of the most overlooked common courtesies in our culture. The good news is that since it is so rare, those who take the time to express their gratitude stand out from the herd.

To say, "Thank you," you need to consider two things:

1. Whom do we need to thank?

2. Who needs to thank them?

Given that most buying decisions involve more than one decision-maker and influencer, you probably need to thank more than one person. The first one needs to go to your key contact. This is the champion that the sales rep worked with to bring the deal through to a close. This needs to be a personal note. Express your gratitude and let them know how much you appreciate what they have done. This note can be handwritten, or you can use a service like SendOutCards to make this easier.

The second thank you needs to go to the CEO, president, or owner of the company. The classiest way to do this is by a letter from the president of your company. In this executive to executive communication, let them know how much you appreciate the opportunity to be of service. Explain your passion for providing an outstanding client experience. Then, share contact information and invite the other executive to reach out if there is any way that they can be of service.

The third set of thank you notes needs to go to the various members of the buying team. These could come from the sales rep or they could come from various people on the sales team. For example, if you have a pre-sales engineer that worked with the client's technical resource, you might have the pre-sales engineer send a thank you card or email to the technical person. The message could welcome them onboard and let them know how to get a hold of the technical resource should any questions arise. Similarly, you could have your financial person send a thank you note or email to the client's financial person.

In today's buying team models, there is usually someone who got out-voted. Your company may not have been their first choice. However, they lost out to the team. While you may know who this person is and may not be happy about them, this is a perfect time to begin to win them over. A thank you note can be a great way to start this process.

2. A Memorable Gift

In addition to the thank you notes, consider how you could make a splash with a memorable gift. This could be something that you give as you deliver your product or service.

I love Cajun food. When you go to a restaurant in Louisiana, it is common for the chef to give a *lagniappe*. This is a French word for something extra. If you ordered blackened redfish, they might throw in a few fried shrimps on the side as a bonus. You leave the restaurant delighted—and full!

One company I worked with had an Otis Spunkmeyer chocolate chip cookie oven in the back. Every new delivery came with a box of freshly baked cookies. While we were delivering technology products that cost tens of thousands of dollars, the thing that the customers remembered most was the cookies. There is nothing wrong with some delicious food to smooth over any inconvenience related to installing and adopting your new product. While each box of cookies costs less than $10, the benefit towards a memorable installation were priceless.

What gifts could you give to your new clients? I like things that will sit on their desk. Few things are more demoralizing to a competitive sales rep than going to meet with a client and seeing that they have a coffee cup or water bottle on their desk branded to your company. While a coffee cup only costs a few dollars, it will usually live in your client's break room and on their desk for years to come.

There are many creative gifts you can send. One of my friends who runs a high-end recruiting agency sends his new clients a box with a fine cigar, a branded box of matches, and a note that says, "Celebrating our new relationship." Another friend sends his new clients a bottle of his favorite Irish whiskey. My banker sent me a beautiful piece of glass art shaped like the state in which we live. Eight years later, this still sits on my desk, reminding me of this bank.

As you consider what kind of memorable gift you could deliver, make sure that it benefits everyone on the buying team. For example, if you decide to give out a branded coffee cup filled with your favorite candy and a "Welcome" note, make sure to bring enough for each member of the team.

What gift could you give to create a memorable experience? The small amount of money you invest can pay ongoing dividends as your clients are reminded of your company.

3. Onboarding Sequence

Email and/or direct mail can play an important role in onboarding new clients. While you are answering common questions about the product they purchased, you can also highlight additional ways your company can help.

With the same email sequence technology used earlier in the prospecting process, you can create a stream of emails that sets the stage for a great client relationship. As you create these emails, make sure they include content about the following items:

Say "Thank You"

You cannot say "Thank You" enough times. I realize you have already sent a personal card, but it is great for the first email that comes from your company to begin and end with "Thank You." Let them know you appreciate the opportunity to serve them.

191

Remind Them Why They Purchased and the Outcomes They Will Get

Buyer's remorse is a real thing. In addition to wondering if they made a bad decision, your client likely faces some challenges as they change the way they do things to accommodate the product or service they purchased. Plus, we all know that even in the best of cases, installing a new product may include some hassles. All of this combines to create a potentially negative situation.

Take the opportunity to remind the client why they purchased your product. In this email sequence, remind them of the outcomes they will enjoy as a result of their decision. Congratulate them for making a good decision. Reassure them that you will be there every step of the way as they implement your product.

Explain How to Work with You

Your onboarding emails can also explain how to work with you. Include helpful links to get support. Show users how to place a service call or enter a support ticket. While you may think your support process is simple, your new client may not understand how to get help. This can lead to frustration. Make this clear in your emails. Also, make sure the support experience on your website and through the phone is streamlined.

Anticipate Challenges

Installing new products or services will create challenges. To minimize the impact of these challenges, sit down with your team and brainstorm the top problems you have experienced when you onboard a client. Obviously, you want to fix the problems that are fixable. However, for the unavoidable challenges, consider using your onboarding email sequence to help new clients anticipate these challenges. For example, if you sell a cloud-based software solution, one of the challenges might be that users cannot find the Web address for your portal. A simple solution might be for the IT department to set up bookmarks in every user's Web browser so that they can find the portal. You could suggest this in the onboarding email.

Help Them Win Over Their Users

Few people like change. Over the years, I have witnessed several end-user rebellions as they bristle about changes that are thrust on them without leadership explaining why the change was made and how the company will benefit.

I have seen cases where the company arrives to install a new product or service and heads start popping up from cubicles and out of doors. "Who are these people? Why are they here? What's changing? Why?"

These rebellions can be disastrous. End users can sabotage the best of sales attempts, leading to unhappy clients and canceled orders.

Think of creative ways that you could win over the end users. You could draft a letter or email that the key decision-maker would use to introduce your company. The letter could explain what is being installed, why the company changed, and list the outcomes the company expects. Links to pages on your website could highlight the product they are buying. The letter should also explain when and how the new system will be deployed, so nobody is surprised.

You can also win over end users by providing training or simply being present to answer questions. Consider how you could conduct a brief onboarding meeting to train end users. This can be done in person, by webinar, or through recorded videos. In addition to training them on how to use the product and get support, make sure to reinforce the outcomes they will enjoy from the new product. Reassure them that you will be there to take care of them.

Recently, I purchased a new cloud service from ClickFunnels.[xiii] The company immediately directed me to their onboarding videos. To thank me for becoming a new client and to ensure I watched the onboarding videos, they offered to send me a free T-shirt if I watched the entire video. This was a smart move. For an investment of less than $10 for a T-shirt, they got me to watch their onboarding video. It reinforced why I bought the service, answered a lot of my questions, and let me know how to get help.

Highlight Additional Outcomes

The primary goal of a great onboarding experience is client satisfaction. The ultimate test of client satisfaction is whether they will purchase additional products from your company.

The payoff from creating an outstanding onboarding experience should be cross-selling additional products and services. While you do not want to be too heavy handed in your cross-selling efforts early in the onboarding process, as you get a few emails into your onboarding sequence, you can start to incorporate messaging about additional services you can provide.

Think about the additional products and services you offer. Build a bridge between the product they purchased and the additional outcomes they could enjoy if they looked to your company for more services. For example, if you sell payroll services and employee benefits, you might let new payroll clients know about the outcomes they could receive by adding your life insurance or long-term care benefits to their services mix. Explain how these can help them recruit top-level talent, retain employees, and boost morale.

Every client communication should include ideas on additional ways they could benefit from working with your company. Some clients will take you up on the offer. However, if you position your message around a sincere desire to deliver additional outcomes to your clients, then even the ones that turn down your offer will feel good about your efforts to help them improve their business.

In the next chapter, we will look at the next two elements in the client management process: periodic business reviews and the client renewal process.

Important Points

1. When is the best time to sell something? Right after they have purchased from you.

2. Find creative ways to say "Thank you."

3. Email and/or direct mail can play an important role in onboarding new clients.

4. Always anticipate challenges.

5. Help management train their staff.

Chapter 11: Cross-Sell Sales Processes - Client Management Part 2

With your clients, one of three things is happening. Some of them are enjoying their experience with your company. These raving fans can be the biggest springboard to your growth, providing referrals and success stories. Their goodwill is your company's biggest asset and you need to leverage this opportunity.

The second group is unhappy with their experience. These dissatisfied clients can slow down and even destroy your success. You need to fix the problem or end those relationships.

The third group are most of your clients; they are somewhere in the middle. They are not upset with the company, but they are not delighted either. Out of sight, out of mind. They own your product or use your service, but rarely hear from you. With a little effort, many of them could become passionate fans. Without any effort, there is a good chance that a negative experience could cause them to slip into the dissatisfied category.

197

The question is: how do you know where your clients are if you do not ask? Tools like client surveys and Net Promoter Scores are good, but only a small percentage of people fill these out. If you want to know how your clients are doing, you need to connect with them.

How often do you connect with your clients? Periodic business reviews provide a consistent cadence of connection. Depending on the type of client and the nature of the relationship, these reviews could happen on a monthly, quarterly, semi-annual, or annual basis. I recommend that, at a minimum, you review your progress with your clients annually.

Why would a client want to take the time to do a periodic business review with you? For the exact same reason that they met with you in the first place: they thought that you might be able to help them achieve their business goals.

During a periodic business review, you need to do five key things:

- Make sure you understand their business goals and desired outcomes.

- Review the outcomes.

- Identify and resolve issues.

- Explore additional opportunities.

- Ask for referrals.

Let's explore each of these.

Business Goals and Desired Outcomes

Remember, people do not buy products; they buy results.
Your relationship with the client began because they believed
your company could help them achieve the outcomes they
desire. Therefore, when you meet with the client to review
their business, you should begin by discussing their business
goals or desired outcomes.

I like to use a PowerPoint presentation to guide a periodic
business review. In this slide deck, the very first slide should
be titled "Business Goals and Desired Outcomes."

If you did a good job during the sales process, you should
already know these goals. During the discussion, start with
the top business goals by saying, "Our commitment to you is
to make sure that we are doing everything possible to help
you achieve your business goals. As we get started today, I
would like to use the first few minutes to make sure I am in
sync with your top-level business goals."

Ask how the company is doing related to the goals. If things
are going well, ask what is driving the success. If they are not
going well, explore what they feel is holding them back. The
answers to these questions will do two things. First, asking
these questions solidifies your position as a consultant,
earning you the "seat at the table" that you desire. Second, the
answers to these questions will often open the door to
opportunities to recommend additional products and services
to help them achieve their goals or overcome the challenges
they face.

If you do not know the client's business goals, leave the slide blank and review them before continuing.

Of course, you can modify this to any situation. If you are selling to a division or a department of a larger organization, instead of asking about business goals, you might ask about their strategic priorities. If you are selling to a small business, you might talk in terms of the vision or future direction of the company. The important thing is to start the discussion by reminding the client (and yourself) that you are there to help them achieve their goals. Otherwise, why would they invest the time to talk with you?

Review the Outcomes

Next, present the outcomes that you are delivering. Make sure to present data that is relevant to the client. Most companies show off a bunch of data to prove they are providing good service. This is okay, but what the client really wants is to see how you are helping them deliver outcomes that are driving them towards their business goals.

For example, I am a partner in a digital marketing and sales enablement company. When our team does quarterly strategy reviews with our clients, we have a ton of data that we can present. We can show website traffic, conversions, social media followers, email opens, and dozens of other data points. If we focus on ourselves, we show data that proves we are delivering on what we said we would do. When we focus on the outcomes that the client wants, the discussion is much different. Our clients want to grow revenue. If we are smart, we show our clients how the growing trends in each of these data points support revenue growth.

Here is another example. Some of our clients sell copiers and printers. During quarterly business reviews, they can present all kinds of data about print usage and service call response time to prove that they are doing a good job. However, the client wants specific business outcomes such as reducing costs, streamlining business processes, and enhancing security. Smart reps structure their review in a way that uses data to show that they are delivering these outcomes.

Identify and Resolve Issues

Most salespeople avoid periodic business reviews because they do not want the inconvenience of dealing with the inevitable issues that arise in any business relationship. Rather than seeing these issues as a problem, though, what if you treat them as an opportunity? Of course, if you do not identify and resolve issues with your key clients, they will fester, and you risk losing this business. However, when you do take the time to identify and resolve issues, you create loyalty. Let's face it, how many companies do this? When you become a company that cares and resolves issues, not only do you cement your relationship, you also open the door to referrals.

Gino Wickman's book, *Traction,* introduces a model that many companies use to improve their operations. In this model, he presents the concept of a Level 10 meeting. The heart of this meeting aims at resolving issues. Wickman recommends what he calls the "IDS Process: Identify, Discuss, and Solve."[xiv] This model can work very well in a periodic business review.

When an issue arises, the first thing to do is identify the root problem. The issue is usually the symptom of the problem. Therefore, you must work with the client to identify the root issue.

> When an issue arises, the first thing to do is to identify the root problem. The issue is usually the symptom of the problem.

Next, discuss potential solutions. Maybe they need more training, or there is a person in the client's organization that is sabotaging the success. Perhaps they could benefit from additional accessories or services to add to what they purchased. Or maybe there are some simple communication issues that could be resolved. In my experience, the solution to issues is rarely complicated.

With all the options on the table, the third step is to solve the problem. Agree with the client on a course of action. Commit to getting things done. Then review the results at your next meeting.

You may be thinking: why would we want to do this? As you work through issues with your clients, you build trust. One of my favorite clients uses the acronym ETR with their sales team: Earn the Right. When you follow through with your clients, you earn the right to cross-sell additional products and services. After all, who would not want to expand their relationship with a company that follows through?

Explore Additional Opportunities

How else can you help your current clients achieve the business outcomes they desire? So far, in your periodic business review, you have discussed their business goals, demonstrated how you are delivering results, and proved that you are committed to solving problems as they arise. It is only logical that you would now look for additional ways to help.

When it comes to cross-selling, strangely, many sales reps feel bad. They think, "I have already asked this person for money; I cannot ask for more yet." However, look at it from the perspective of the client. Remember, they did not buy a product from you; they bought an outcome. Now that you are demonstrating your ability to deliver outcomes, why wouldn't your clients want to get more outcomes from a vendor that they know, like, and trust?

The key to cross-selling is to focus on outcomes, not the product. Refer back to the client's business goals and suggest ways that they could achieve their goals faster. You could say, "Earlier, we talked about your goal to improve investor confidence, as well as your challenge in complying with new privacy regulations that come into effect next year. Would you be open to exploring an idea that could help with these areas?" When the client says "Yes" to a question like this, you have received an open invitation to explore additional offerings with them.

Ask for Referrals

Here is where your hard work really pays off. When you take great care of your clients, you earn the right to ask for referrals. The best time to ask for a referral is after you have demonstrated to your client that you care enough to come back and ensure that they are receiving the outcomes you promised.

Most sales reps struggle with referrals because they have not yet earned the right. Periodic business reviews create favorable moments where you have earned the right.

At the end of your business review, let your client know how much you appreciate their business. Reiterate your commitment to follow through and make sure they realize the outcomes they desire. Then, let them know that you have made a strategic decision to spend most of your time working with clients. As a result, you need their help to grow your business.

Most good clients will be willing to help. After all, you have demonstrated your willingness to work for them. They feel a healthy obligation to return the favor.

One common way to ask is, "Who else do you know that could benefit from our services?" However, my experience has shown that this usually results in the client saying, "Hmm. I'm not sure. Let me think about it and get back to you." Rarely, though, will the client do so.

Instead, prepare for the referral question by doing your homework. Check the prospect's social media profile and see who they are connected with that you would like to meet. Are there people in your target accounts? Then, you can ask, "One of the companies I would really like to work with is Acme Corp. I noticed that you are connected to their CFO. Would you feel comfortable bridging an introduction?" This specific type of ask usually ends in success. If they say, "No, I do not know the CFO very well," you can follow up with a question like, "No worries. Are there other CFOs you know who could benefit from the outcomes we deliver?"

These referrals are the golden ticket to driving net-new business. Amazingly, the more you focus on periodic business reviews with your current client, the more they will help you expand.

Renewal Process

Hopefully, you have a product, service, or solution that needs to be renewed or upgraded on a regular cycle. Much of my career was spent in the technology world where the products were leased. The beauty of this arrangement is that the contract expiration created an event that had a sense of urgency. Similarly, my iPhone is on a program that makes it eligible for an upgrade every year.

If you do not have a predictable upgrade program, I recommend that you try to find ways to incorporate this into your business. If you do have an upgrade program, I want you to think about how you could make this process more efficient and more profitable.

Without offering additional outcomes to your clients, it's likely that they'll pay less each time you ask them to renew. I saw this happen in the office technology world. Even though each new generation of the products we were selling had more features that could help clients drive business outcomes, sales tended to renew at a lower cost. Instead of creating a value proposition that grew revenue, the, "You should renew so you can lower your payment," value proposition led to steadily declining revenues per client.

In contrast, Apple has managed to sustain and grow its revenue per device, even in a saturated market. Each year, I join tens of millions of people who enthusiastically upgrade to the new model. My last iPhone retailed for over $1,000, a significant increase over the retail price of the previous year's model. All of this happened in a marketplace where most competitors continue to drop their average selling prices in the race to the bottom.

How do companies like Apple maintain and grow their average selling price? They do it by communicating the value of the outcomes they will deliver. Instead of building a value proposition around being less expensive than last year, Apple's value proposition says, "We're going to give you new features that will make your life more fun and productive—all for just a small amount more than you are currently paying."

On top of this, Apple continues to add new services like Music, News, and Games. So, along with my more expensive iPhone, I have found myself subscribing to monthly services that I love. Because of this, Apple has now developed a multi-billion dollar a year services business.

How could you do the same thing in your business? You could support the upgrade and renewal process by messaging the outcomes your newer products and services could deliver.

Think about your company's renewal or upgrade experience from the perspective of a client. For many companies, the sales rep calls up and says, "We need to meet soon because your lease is coming to an end." At the meeting, the sales rep reviews the client's current needs, talks about what is new, and hopefully gets an upgrade. In this short meeting, the client does not have the opportunity to understand the benefits of the new technology fully. As a result, the conversation ends up being about the price. Since the conversation is about price, the client also brings in some competitors to get price quotes.

Instead, what if you set the stage for the upgrade meeting with a series of messages around the outcomes that the newer products and services could deliver? These messages could include testimonials or success stories from clients who have adopted the new technology. By the time the sales rep arrives, the client could be enthusiastic about the new offering, much like the way I cannot wait to get to the Apple store when a new iPhone is launched.

The same technology that your sales team uses for prospecting could be used to create upgrade sequences for each of your core product areas. These sequences could be triggered by upgrade dates in your CRM.

To further support the upgrade process, consider how you could equip your sales team with presentations and sales tools that communicate the benefits of your newer offerings. Rather than thinking about how you could decrease your clients' expenditures, think about how you could deliver additional outcomes for a marginal increase in your costs to the client.

One of the key components of the business review is the relationship that you create. Today's business economy is based on how you care for your clients. They want to know that it is a partnership, and not just about dollar signs.

A key part of relationships is communication, which we will talk about in the next chapter.

Important Points

1. How do you know if your clients are happy with your product or service if you do not ask?

2. Are you setting business goals and desired outcomes, reviewing the outcomes, identifying and resolving issues, exploring additional opportunities, and asking for referrals?

Darrell Amy

Chapter 12: Cross-Sell Marketing Processes - Client Communication

How often do your current clients hear from your company? When they do, what message do they receive?

Sadly, most companies do not communicate regularly with their clients. The only time the client hears from the company is when something has gone wrong or when it is time to renew a contract. Neither of these scenarios generates goodwill.

Instead of waiting until something goes wrong, or the client needs to spend money, what if you could develop a consistent cadence of communication with your clients when they are happy? What if the content of this communication included helpful messages about how they could receive additional outcomes from the products and services you offer? Not only would this build goodwill towards your company, creating higher client loyalty, it would also set the stage for cross-selling additional products and services.

In this section, we will explore four components of a client communication strategy. First, you need to segment your

211

clients based on their cross-sell potential. This ensures that the messages you send are relevant to them. Second, create a client loyalty program for your ideal clients. Third, establish a regular communication cadence. Fourth, host events to build personal relationships with your clients.

Remember, all of this is fueled by a focused message. The work you do in creating outcome-focused website pages, blog articles, downloadable reports, and social media posts will pay off as you use this content in your client communication strategy to earn the right to be seen as a trusted business partner.

1. Segment Your Clients

First, you need to segment your clients. Most companies skip this step. As a result, they end up sending generic messages to their whole client base. These messages get tuned out and you miss the opportunity to build credibility, confidence, and trust with your clients.

The goal is to cross-sell additional products and services to your client base. In support of this goal, you should be able to pull lists of clients that are targets. Let's explore how to do this.

First, create a list of all your product and service categories. For each category, identify the types of clients that would be a great fit for these offerings. There is a good chance that not every client is a candidate for all your products or services. Therefore, it is worth your time to segment your client base by the offerings.

For example, if you sell employee benefits, your categories might include payroll services, health insurance, life insurance, management training, and HR consulting. Maybe small clients are too small for your management training and HR consulting. Larger clients that have finance departments might be a good fit for payroll services. By segmenting your client base, you can avoid sending clients messages about services that are not relevant to them.

> By segmenting your client base, you can avoid sending clients messages about services that are not relevant to them.

You might also have offerings that apply to different vertical market segments. Maybe you have different cloud solutions for education, legal issues, and healthcare. Maybe your different offerings are based on the location of your client.

Next, go through your client base and identify the ones that are targets for each of your offerings. Each client should be clearly marked with the products and services for which they are a good fit.

You can do this in your CRM and your marketing automation platform. This will allow you to easily filter lists of targets for each of your offerings. When a sales rep pulls up a client record in the CRM, they should be able to see what products and services the client is currently using or could be using. When you launch a marketing campaign, you should be able to target it to the right people.

You need to do this exercise with your client base each time your company adds a new product or service category. This ensures you get the message out quickly to support the growth of this new area.

2. Create a Client Loyalty Program

American Express is famous for their slogan, "Membership has its privileges." When you get one of their cards, you are not just a cardholder, you are a member.

In my work with clients and speaking at conferences, I routinely endure the hassle of flying. As an American Express member, I get more than a credit card. For a relatively small annual fee, I am part of their Platinum program. This gives me access to express security screening, airport lounges, Wi-Fi on the plane, discounts on Uber, status at major hotel chains, and insurance on rental cars. I also get points for my purchases.

American Express goes even further by offering additional products and services for my business. As a member, I get discounts on travel through their travel agency. I can secure lines of credit through their merchant account loan program. They also have partnerships with companies that allow me to take advantage of discounts.

I like to talk about American Express because of the benefits I receive for being a member. When I travel, I look forward to connections in an airport that has a Centurion Lounge. Follow me on Instagram (@darrellamy) or Twitter (@darrell_amy) and you will see me sharing pictures from these amazing venues! This creates free advertising for American Express, helping them grow their business.

Every day, I receive offers in the mail for new business credit cards. If it were only about a credit card, it would be easy to change providers. However, with these perks that make my life and business better, it would be very hard to get me to change.

What privileges do your ideal clients receive? If you could add perks that made your client experience more memorable, not only could you increase client loyalty, you could also cross-sell more services, helping you grow revenue. Best of all, these raving-fan clients can become the source of positive PR that can drive your growth.

The following are a few ideas to enhance your ideal client experience and build loyalty:

Perks

American Express offers many perks to their ideal clients. What perks could you offer to your ideal clients?

You likely already do a lot of things for your best clients like offering priority support. The problem is that you probably do not tell your clients about these perks.

Make a list of all the perks you already have. Then, consider others you could provide to your ideal clients and prospects.

Recently, I was working with a technology company. When I first asked about what perks they provide, they said that they didn't have a perks program. However, when I dug deeper, we made a list of eight ways they were already going above and beyond the norm for their ideal clients. Most of these were benefits their competitors did not offer.

Once you make a list of things you currently do, think about things that you could do to improve your client experience. You might look at loyalty programs from other industries to get ideas. Or, you might ask some of your current clients what they would value.

Bundling

My insurance company, State Farm, does a great job with bundling. They understand that it costs five to twenty-five times more to get a new client than to sell to a current one. They take the money they save on landing a new client and use it to create discounts for bundling home, auto, personal liability, and life insurance. As a consumer, I could shop around for each of these items.

This is a smart strategy because it keeps me loyal. I know that if I picked another provider, I would lose the discount on my existing products and the cost would go up, thus offsetting any savings I might achieve by switching vendors for one product. Second, I do not want to have to pay an additional bill each month. I like to keep things simple. The only way out of the relationship is to move all my insurance and that would be a huge hassle.

How could you bundle your products and services in a way that benefits your ideal clients? You know that it costs you something to land a new client. Why not apply some of this cost to provide discounts to your current clients who buy more services from you?

216

Rewards Points

Whoever invented frequent flier miles was a genius. I love the ability to travel around the world, but I think we can all admit that the process of flying is a nuisance. However, as I endure the frustration of airport security, boarding, disembarking, and lost luggage, I know in the back of my mind that my suffering is being rewarded with frequent flyer miles. As I bank these miles, I know that someday I will use them to take my wife on a vacation to Europe or the Caribbean.

When it comes time to book a flight, there is one airline that I prefer simply because I am gathering miles on this carrier. Within reason, I will go out of my way to book flights with this company, sometimes even paying more for tickets just to get the miles. Over the years, I have earned status that gets me creature comforts such as access to premium seating, free bag checks, and the occasional upgrade to first class.

Points are everywhere. They are almost expected. I get points with my grocery store, credit cards, gas station, hardware store, oil change shop, and several local restaurants. These programs affect my buying habits, giving me the nudge to choose one vendor over another.

Creating a points program is an exercise in math. First, decide what kind of discount you would be willing to provide for current clients to apply to additional products and services for your company. Second, equate your points to that discount amount.

For example, to use round numbers, let's assume you are willing to extend a 10% discount to clients that would purchase additional products and services. For every $100 a client spends, they would get points equivalent to $10. If you gave the client ten points for every dollar they spent, their 1,000 points would be worth $10 toward future purchases.

You might be concerned that a client could accumulate enough points to get an additional product for free. Keep in mind that you decided to allocate 10% of their spending toward additional products. In essence, they have been pre-paying for additional services, whether they use the points or not.

Since this is clearly not an accounting book, you will want to involve your financial team as you decide how to roll out a program like this. From a revenue growth perspective, however, a points program creates a proven way to drive client loyalty.

Affiliate Partnerships

Creating affiliate relationships with companies that complement your service is another way to build loyalty while also creating additional revenue streams. Intuit has QuickBooks Online, which provides cloud-based accounting software to businesses. While Intuit specializes in accounting, they have recognized that their clients need additional products and services related to bookkeeping such as check printing and lines of credit. Although Intuit does not provide either of these products directly, they have formed partnerships with companies that print checks and lend money.

As an Intuit client, you get a discount on these items. I would guess that Intuit also gets a commission on the back end from these partners. Not only do these partnerships create a seamless experience for their clients, they also create a barrier to leaving. If a company uses Intuit in a loan partnership, then changing accounting software could also mean losing access to a line of credit.

What products and services complement your offerings? Consider how you could form relationships with reputable companies in these areas. Not only will this create perks for your clients, it could also add incremental revenue while helping ensure client loyalty.

Package Up an Ideal Client Loyalty Program

Once you establish your perks, bundles, points, and partnerships, package this up into a client loyalty program.

First, give your program a name. You might call it the "Priority Club" or "Platinum Program." There is no need to get too clever here. Just make sure that your clients know they are getting something special.

Next, take that name and create a logo or badge. Make sure this matches your current brand.

Finally, take all your benefits and create an attractive brochure. Sales reps can share this with clients during their periodic business review meetings. This can also be used during the sales process to differentiate you from the competition.

You can get creative in how you use this. You might create a special support phone number for your priority clients. Simple gifts like coffee cups, pens, and T-shirts make people feel special. If you sell products, you might put the priority program logo on the product itself.

As clients begin enjoying the benefits of a client loyalty program, it makes it harder for them to leave. It also creates the type of experience that generates referrals, helping you grow even more.

3. Establish a Regular Communication Cadence

With your client list segmented and a perks program in place, you now have the ingredients for an effective communication strategy with your clients.

Over the years, I have watched many companies use email and direct mail incorrectly. When it comes to non-customers, they do not hesitate to blast out emails and carpet bomb prospects with direct mail, but when it comes to their clients, many companies are reluctant to send messages, fearing that they will annoy them. Ironically, your prospects have not given you permission to communicate with them, while your clients have.

I understand the sentiment of not wanting to annoy your clients, but this does not mean you should not communicate with them. You have a relationship. You also have additional ways you can help. You should share these ideas.

The issue is not whether to communicate; the issue is *what* you communicate and how you do it. If you share ideas and insights that help your clients get better outcomes, your message is relevant. You can share it with confidence.

With the incredible volume of information and the massive number of messages in today's world, we have all become very good at filtering out noise. While many see this as a negative, I challenge you to see it as a positive. Our elaborate filters cause things that matter to us to stand out.

For example, I recently purchased a home with a pool in the backyard. While the pool looks beautiful, I have to admit that when it comes to taking care of one, I do not know very much. The mix of chemicals and machinery that keep the water crystal clear is a mystery to me. Right now, I am hungry for information on how to take care of a pool. Throughout the day, I filter out thousands of emails, ads, and direct mail pieces. However, if something crosses my radar related to how to take care of a pool, that company will have my attention.

Within the context of their business, every client has a list of pressing issues. Their message filter ignores most of the static specifically so that they can focus on incoming information that could help them solve their problems.

> If you understand the common problems that your clients face, you can tailor your messages to address them.

If you understand the common problems that your clients face, you can tailor your messages to address them. This will get their attention. If a given message does not address the client's top-of-mind problem, it is okay. As they are filtering out the message, they will notice that you are sending information to help your clients solve problems. This will continue to build your relationship with the client. Chances are, they will see your efforts and think your company could be helpful in the future.

As you think about sending out messages to your clients to help them address business challenges, allow me to add an important caution: Resist the urge to blast out the same message to your entire client base. For a message to be relevant, it needs to address the desired business outcomes of the recipient. This is why the first step in creating a client communication strategy is to segment your client list. Then, you need to understand the outcomes and challenges of each segment. Craft your message to this segment. It's likely that not every product or service you sell is relevant to all your clients.

In segmenting your clients by cross-sell potential, you can send useful ideas to each segment. Unless all your clients are the same, do not take the lazy way out, blasting the same message to every client.

As you do this, make sure to pay special attention to the headlines. We have been trained to scan headlines of articles and subject lines of emails to determine if they are worth our attention. When we see a headline that relates to an outcome that we want to achieve, we read the article. We do this as we browse websites and scroll through social media. We also do this as we scan our email inboxes.

The key to getting attention is to focus your effort on where the reader is focused: the headline or subject line. For blog articles, this is the title of the blog. For emails, this is the subject line of the email. For social media posts, this includes the first sentence of the post along with the headline of the article you are sharing. For postcards, this includes the headline on the front and back of the card. For special reports and eBooks, this includes the title. For landing pages, this includes the headline.

Each one must be relevant to the buyer. While a quick Google search will give you many great online resources to help you write effective headlines, the foundational principle is simple: every headline needs to address an outcome that is important to the buyer.

Let's consider several ways that you can communicate.

Targeted Email

Despite abuse by spammers, email remains one of the most effective ways to communicate with your clients; however, you can still misuse it.

There are two ways to do so. The first is to send email too often. While the frequency depends on the type of products you sell, as a rule of thumb, I recommend not sending more than one email a week to your clients. The second way businesses abuse email and direct mail is less obvious. They do so by sending irrelevant messages to their clients. When this happens, you get tuned out and clients hit the "Junk" button in their email program.

When it comes to public speaking, the common advice is: "Be clear, be brief, and be gone." Your email messages should follow this advice. Keep them short.

> Take the time to distill your message, cutting out the fluff. Longer is not better.

Many people now check email on their smartphones. Ideally, you should be able to fit your email message on the screen of a phone. If it must be longer than that, your recipient must have an idea of what you are talking about in the part that fits on the screen, otherwise, most recipients will not scroll down.

Short messages are harder to write than longer ones. Take the time to distill your message, cutting out the fluff. Longer is not better.

When your email and direct mail messages are relevant to the client, you earn the right to get their attention. To make sure this happens, segment your email lists in a way that allows you to send messages that are relevant.

When you send bulk emails, make sure you have permission. Since we are discussing sending emails to current clients, there is an existing business relationship in place that gives implied permission. The current trend is for governments to pass laws that protect personal information. Because of this, I recommend two things. First, understand your local laws as they relate to email. Second, have an email sending platform that helps you comply with these laws.

As wonderful (and free) as email is, only a percentage of your messages will get to the inbox. Years of abuse by spammers and cyber thugs have driven many companies to employ rigorous email-filtering programs. As a result, only a percentage of your messages will get read. That is why I recommend you look to multiple communication channels to communicate with your clients including direct mail, retargeting, and social media.

Targeted Direct Mail

Everyone has experienced sorting through the mail. Much like email, we look at every piece of direct mail and decide if it is relevant. To make the cut, a letter, postcard, or magazine either needs to be from a company with whom we do business and/or it needs to be relevant to the outcomes we want.

Many direct mail companies try to be sneaky to get you to open their mail and try to disguise their pieces as important government documents. They put ridiculous things on the envelope like "Important information for the recipient only" or "Tampering with mail is a felony."

Do not play these games. Instead, make sure that your company is clearly identified on the mail piece. After all, you are their vendor.

Just like email, make sure the headline of the mail piece addresses an outcome that the client wants. Personally, I like postcards because you can put a bold headline on the front and back of the card.

As with email messages, be brief. Whether you send a postcard or a traditional letter, the fewer words, the better.

With direct mail, the cadence is likely more limited by your budget. Once or maybe twice a month should be sufficient. Fortunately, there are many printing and mail houses that make the process of sending direct mail to your clients simple and affordable.

Customized Web Content

Do your clients come to your website to interact with your company? If so, this is a great place to cross-sell, sharing additional ways you can help.

If you have a support section on your website, take a look at the support pages. Could you add graphics or content that provides helpful information to your clients? Graphics can link to pages on your website explaining the benefits of additional services. Helpful blog articles could showcase ways they would benefit from your company.

Most support systems also send out confirmation and follow-up emails for a service interaction. These are great opportunities to communicate since clients usually give more attention to a support email than a marketing email.

Along with customizing the support section of your website, you may be able to customize the content on your home page and other parts of your website. Certain platforms allow you to alter content based on the IP address of the visitor to your website. Basically, this means that clients in your database could see different graphics on your website than non-clients. This could apply to your home page graphics. It could also apply to the calls-to-action on your blog. Use such strategies to promote additional products and services to your client base.

4. Hosting Events

Events create a time for you to build relationships with your clients outside of their office. They also provide a great forum for cross-selling additional products and services. Events can range from informal gatherings like a sporting event or charity fundraiser to more educational functions like a lunch-and-learn or webinar. Each of these forums provides a great opportunity to cross-sell.

If your company participates in informal gatherings like inviting clients to a sporting event, consider how you could share information at that event. You could have banner stands or video displays around the venue showcasing the different ways you help clients achieve outcomes. You might even include client testimonials with short quotes about how they have benefitted from different products and services you would like to cross-sell. You could also include customized drinking cups with your logo and a list of all the different things you sell.

More formal events provide a forum for education. Your clients are always looking for ways to improve their businesses. Offering seminars that help them learn how other businesses are achieving outcomes is a great way to cross-sell while building client loyalty.

Educational events can be very powerful. Marketing guru, Jay Abraham, author of *Getting Everything You Can Out of All You've Got*, talks about the paradox of knowledge: the more you know about a topic, the more questions you have. When you educate your clients, they begin to have more questions. Where do they go to get the questions answered? They go to the person (or company) that educated them.

What do your clients want to learn about? It all goes back to outcomes: they want to learn how they can make their business better. Like your other marketing and sales content, your events should share strategies that your clients can use to get the outcomes they want.

Do not make your event presentations a product pitch. Instead, begin with the goals and challenges that the audience faces. Then, build the bridge to how they can achieve their goals and solve their problems. Show specific examples of how other companies have done this to build credibility. At the end, offer to meet with any of the attendees who want to go deeper.

Much like email and direct mail, be brief. Nobody wants to sit through a two-hour PowerPoint slide dump. Keep your sessions under 45 minutes. Ideally, you could present for 20–30 minutes and then open the floor for discussion.

There are many ways to host educational events. Lunch-and-learns allow people to get out of the office and enjoy a meal while learning something. You can host these at your office or local restaurants.

Open houses are a great way to bring clients into your office. This annual function could include educational sessions on various topics. Make your guests comfortable with food and drink. You could even bridge this into an after-hours networking event.

Along with live events, I recommend you develop a regular schedule of webinars. These allow your clients and prospects to learn in the comfort of their own office. As a bonus, you can record these webinars and post them on your website.

Should you invite non-clients to your events? Absolutely. However, I recommend that you position such occasions as client events. Many companies host events for prospects that seem very salesy. Nobody wants to come to these types of gatherings.

Make it more like a country club. If your friend who is a member of the country club invites you to play golf, you feel special as a guest. When prospects come, they get the sense that they are special guests. They will also get to network with your current clients and team members, providing a great forum for building trust.

Communication is the key to solid business relationships. Make it a priority to not only communicate with your clients more, but also show them that they are a valued part of your business.

Important Points

1. How often do your current clients hear from your company? When they do, what message do they receive?

2. Are you segmenting your clients, creating a client loyalty program, establishing a regular communication cadence, and hosting events?

Darrell Amy

Section 4: Build Your Engine

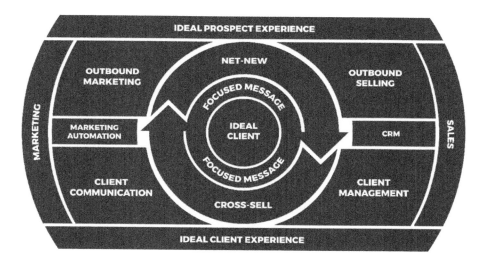

As both a football and marketing aficionado, my favorite television event of the year is the Super Bowl. I find myself riveted to the TV screen for both the game and the commercials. In the middle of all the action, it can be hard to find a break to go refill my plate with more wings!

In the Super Bowl, like all sports, the most important thing is the score. Without the score, we would never know who won the game! The problem with the score is that you do not find out the winner until the end of the game. That is why there are dozens of statistics behind the score. For the team, you can see the total offensive yards, number of turnovers, and third-down conversion rates. For individual players, you will see things like quarterback efficiency or yards per carry. All these statistics point toward the final score.

Your company also keeps score. Earlier, we established the two metrics for revenue growth: number of clients and revenue per client. Behind these two numbers are statistics for each area of your Revenue Growth Engine that drive your growth.

In sports, players are evaluated and paid based on their results. If a player delivers great statistics, they can probably look forward to a lucrative contract. With an all-star roster, the team ownership expects to get a positive ROI of ticket sales for their salary investment. Once their statistics slip, players get traded.

Your marketing and sales efforts are very similar. Things that are working to drive revenue should get a bigger budget. Areas that aren't working should either be improved or scrapped.

You will never know what to invest in, what to coach, and what to scrap if you do not have a system to measure and track revenue growth statistics.

In this section, we will explore the data you can track and how to interpret it. This helps you understand which areas of your engine are performing and which areas need some attention.

Chapter 13: Set Your Budget

In *The 7 Habits of Highly Effective People*, Stephen Covey talks about four quadrants of tasks. One axis is "urgent/not urgent," and the other axis is "important/not important."[xv] Creating a Revenue Growth Engine, budgeting for the technology, training, and tracking success all take time. There are always urgent things that hinder these efforts. Your Revenue Growth Engine is a "not urgent but important" category. It is worthy of your time and budget.

This chapter is for the CFO and finance managers who are wondering if the investment is worthwhile. It is also an informative chapter for the creative-minded marketing associate and the relationship-focused sales leaders because getting and keeping the resources you need requires the ability to justify the return on the investment.

Budget: How Much Should We Spend?

Some companies have small budgets for marketing and sales enablement. Others have no budget for these areas. In either case, adding any expenses may seem counterintuitive in a world where most companies are trying to trim overhead.

To use the analogy of a vehicle, no engine will run without some investment in fuel and maintenance. Your Revenue Growth Engine is the same. You are going to need to allocate some funds for it if you want it to perform.

Your Revenue Growth Engine is an investment, not an expense. Fortunately, as you build your engine, you create an infrastructure that will serve your company for years to come. For example, the investment you make to create a focused message on your website, blog, and social media channels will not only help your company increase revenue immediately by communicating a meaningful value proposition, but this content will also remain on these channels for years to come. Similarly, the budget you invest in building calls-to-action to convert website visitors into leads should yield returns long after the financial period in which you paid to have the content built. The same goes for your sales sequences, sales collateral, onboarding process, and renewal process.

I have noticed that the financially-minded among us tend to think that marketing and sales enablement should be easy to do and not take much time. A low budget for marketing staff, agency partners, and technology platforms may be less expensive in the short term, but you will miss out on the long-term benefits. So, how do you set a budget for something unknown? You need to factor in four cost areas: strategy, development, management, and technology.

Strategy

The strategy budget is important. Randomly choosing marketing and sales tactics based on the latest conference you attended, or advice from the local advertising sales rep, is a formula to waste money. Before chasing the latest shiny marketing or sales object, you need a strategy.

Your revenue growth strategy needs to be thought through as a team and clearly documented. Like all good strategies, it should begin with your business goals. Then, it should document your plan to execute and the data you will use to measure success.

Most companies have separate marketing and sales plans. They then wonder why it is so hard to get marketing and sales aligned. A revenue growth strategy includes both marketing and sales with the focused aim of growing revenue.

Creating a strategy typically involves bringing in a third party that helps you develop a plan that aligns your marketing and sales efforts to achieve your business goals. Having led many Revenue Growth Workshops, I have seen the value of pulling executive, marketing, and sales teams into the same room to create a revenue growth strategy. Once the plan is in motion, this same partner can help measure success and recommend adjustments based on data.

Development

Your Revenue Growth Engine will always require some development. You will need to apply a significant amount of effort to this area to present a focused message. After you create your ideal client profile and your ideal client experience map, you will need to update your marketing and sales material so that they all communicate the same focused message. You also need to budget for developing the processes for the cylinders of your Revenue Growth Engine.

Development never stops. You can trim back your budget after your message is deployed and the cylinders of your growth engine are in place, but there will be ongoing needs for development. At a minimum, you need to plan to update your website and social media continually. However, with change being the reality of today's business world, you need to make sure that your Revenue Growth Engine has the available budget to adapt.

Management

You should plan a continuous budget to run and maintain your Revenue Growth Engine. For marketing, you need a lead manager that responds to leads and qualifies them. This person or team should have their eye on your digital platforms, continually looking for sales opportunities. You need a marketing coordinator ensuring that your website is fresh with blog articles and executing your social media strategy. Someone will need to execute your client communication strategy. Some tasks will be sending targeted messages and offers to segments of your client base, arranging and hosting onsite events and webinars.

For sales enablement, you need a sales coordinator to manage data in your CRM. The task will include ensuring the data is clean and updated, working with the sales team to make sure the pipeline and forecast are correct. Once a deal closes, their role is to make certain the deal is accurately attributed back to a lead source so that you can make informed decisions about your return on investment. The sales coordinator will make sure that the new client onboarding and renewal processes happen consistently; they will hold the sales team accountable to ensure that periodic business reviews happen.

You may think these are tasks for the sales manager, but sales managers are more relational and should spend their time recruiting, developing, and coaching sales reps. The skills that make a sales manager good at their job are typically not administrative. Support your sales manager by letting them do their job unhindered by providing a sales coordinator.

Technology

Technology also needs to be part of your budget. Our cloud-based world has all but eradicated the large capital expenses for CRM software and servers. This does not mean that you can get away without budgeting for marketing and sales enablement technology. You should expect to spend more on technology today than you ever have.

In our cloud-based world, these investments are typically monthly subscriptions where you can add or delete users as necessary, making it highly scalable.

To work on these platforms, you need to make sure your sales reps have computers, tablets, and phones that are connected to the Internet, allowing them to operate in a mobile environment. If you are interested in learning about the technologies needed, I have created a companion guide, *Revenue Growth Technologies* www.RevenueGrowthEngine.net/technology

While the tech landscape continues to shift, this book will give you a framework to make good technology decisions.

Setting a Budget

Strategy, development, management, and technology all require a budget. How do you work these costs into your financial model? Here are a few ideas to consider.

Years ago, when my marketing agency first started offering inbound marketing services, we were asking our clients to significantly increase their marketing budget to build an infrastructure to capture buyers who were doing online research. My question to these business owners was this: "How many sales representatives are you planning to hire this year?" When they answered the question, my response was always the same: "I want my budget to be one of your sales reps."

Every day, companies roll the dice on hiring new sales reps. When I was a manager, by the time we recruited, onboarded, trained, and coached a sales rep, it cost an average of $55,000. We made this investment knowing that the chances were two out of every three reps would leave within the first eighteen months. Why did we do this? We did not know a better way.

As you set your budget, instead of just hiring more sales reps, why not take some of that budget and put it toward building and maintaining your Revenue Growth Engine? The investment you make in your Revenue Growth Engine provides the foundation for sales enablement that should make your sales team more effective.

Recently, I was watching a documentary on the history of Coca Cola. As far back as the late 1800s, the company invested 20 percent of its revenue in advertising. You do not need to allocate that much. However, you do need to allocate some of your revenue to fund your growth engine.

The Small Business Association recommends that businesses spend between 5 and 7 percent of their budget on marketing.

The Small Business Association recommends that businesses spend between 5 and 7 percent of their budget on marketing. While these budget amounts vary widely between industries, if your marketing and sales enablement budget is below 5 percent of revenue, you are getting off cheap. The question to ask is this: If we increased our budget for marketing and sales enablement by 1 to 2 percent of annual revenue, could we at least recover that cost from additional sales? The answer should be, "Yes!"

For a $10-million company, this increase to the marketing budget would mean an additional $100,000–$200,000 per year. If this budget was invested strategically in building a Revenue Growth Engine, would it yield at least that much in additional gross profit from net-new sales and cross-selling additional clients? If this company were able to grow both net-new sales while cross-selling additional clients at a modest rate of 10–15 percent, then it could double revenue in less than three years. In this case, strategic investment in growth is the smart choice.

If your Revenue Growth Engine is in poor shape, it may take some additional investment to get things in motion. Where will we get these funds? Look at your entire budget and ask yourself this question: "Will this expense drive growth?" I am sure that having new conference room furniture would be nice, but if your Revenue Growth Engine needs serious work, consider delaying other expenditures in the short term to build the infrastructure that will enable long-term growth. As your Revenue Growth Engine starts humming along, there will be a bigger budget for that conference room—and other expenses for your growing company.

Recovering the Costs

When you invest, you need to recover your costs. While the ultimate goal is revenue growth, there are some ways to recover your marketing and sales enablement expenses. Most of the investments you will make in this area are monthly expenses for people, partners, and technology; but it is possible to get things in motion without large capital expenses and then recover these costs as you go. Here are a few ideas about how you can do this.

1. Load Your Sales Costs

Marketing and sales enablement are a cost of doing business. If you sell a product, you have the cost of shipping, warehousing, and delivering that product. That cost gets built into the sales price that you pass on to your sales team. It can be buried in the price of the product or you itemize it separately in things like "shipping and handling."

Calculating this is fairly simple. Let's say that your annual sales are $10 million, and your marketing and sales enablement budget is $200,000. Your sales load would be 2 percent ($200,000 budget/$10,000,000 sales). Over time, you might add a 2 percent buffer to the sales cost for your products.

2. Cost per Deal

Another way to recover this value is to add a flat cost to every deal. If you close 2,000 deals per year and have a $200,000 budget, then your cost per deal is $100 ($200,000 budget/2,000 deals). You could add a $100 sales charge to each deal.

3. Lead Charge

Sales reps should be prospecting for their own new opportunities. However, when they are handed a lead, the company has invested in creating that prospect. In this case, it is not unreasonable to pass a lead charge on to the sales rep. The lead charge could be a flat amount for the lead, deducted from the commission when they close the sale. Or, it could be a slightly lower commission rate for deals from leads created by the marketing team.

4. Adjust Your Compensation Plan

As a former sales representative and sales manager, I know that changing compensation plans can cause many challenges. When you change your compensation plan, factor the increased marketing and sales costs into the calculation. You can adjust a compensation plan by increasing the quota. Nobody likes a quota increase. However, with a strategy in place to generate more net-new business and cross-sell current clients, you also have some good news to deliver along with the bad news of a higher quota. With your Revenue Growth Engine operating at peak performance, over time you should expect more out of your sales team.

Another way to adjust compensation is to leave the base commission plan the same but modify the bonus plan. Years ago, when I was a sales representative for an office equipment company, we had to sell fax machines. Nobody on the sales team wanted to sell fax machines because they were a hassle and had a lower sales value than other products we sold. To motivate us, the company decided to gate our bonus. We received a 2 percent bonus on our total revenue if we hit our fax quota. If we did not, the bonus was 0.5 percent. This incentive changed our behavior. We always hit our quota so we could get a higher bonus on our total dollar volume.

You might also factor this into the qualifications for your annual President's Club trip or sales contests. Instead of just having a sales dollar target, try including separate targets for net-new and cross-sell business. Also, include your marketing team, rewarding them for hitting their lead target.

Consider providing incentives for both net-new and cross-sell deals. If you are struggling with cross-selling, create a bonus plan that is based on a cross-sell quota. For example, you could gate your bonus based on achieving a minimum amount of sales. The bonus will drive additional revenue and profit, which can help offset the investment in your Revenue Growth Engine while you are growing it.

Hopefully, this chapter has helped you see that you can effectively budget and cover the costs of incorporating a Revenue Growth Engine into your business. In the next chapter, we are going to look at how to calculate your return on investment to ensure that your engine is working properly.

Important Points

1. Creating a Revenue Growth Engine, budgeting for the technology, training, and tracking success, all take time. There are always urgent things that hinder these efforts. Your Revenue Growth Engine may not be urgent, but it's an important category.

2. To use the analogy of a vehicle, no engine will run without some investment in fuel and maintenance. Your Revenue Growth Engine is the same. You must allocate an ongoing budget for it if you want it to perform.

3. Your revenue growth strategy needs to be thought through as a team and clearly documented.

4. Your Revenue Growth Engine will always require some development. You will need to apply a significant amount of effort to this area to present a focused message.

5. Most of the investments you will make in this area are monthly expenses for people, partners, and technology. It is possible to get things in motion without large capital expenses and then recover these costs as you go.

Chapter 14: Measure Results

A s I mentioned before, I am a football fan, especially college football. As I write this chapter, the college football season is about to begin. While I enjoy the dynamics of the game from the fun of tailgating to the energy of the stadium, what I enjoy most is the celebration when my team wins.

To determine who is winning, every game has a scoreboard. Through the four quarters of the game, the scoreboard tracks the touchdowns, field goals, and occasional safety.

The final score for the game of business is revenue growth. As we have discussed, behind the total revenue number are two key metrics:

Number of Clients: This measures the effectiveness of the net-new half of your Revenue Growth Engine. This number is simple: how many current clients do you have that are regularly sending you money?

Revenue Per Client: This measures the effectiveness of the cross-selling half of your Revenue Growth Engine. This number is simple as well: what is the total revenue for a given period (trailing year, quarter, or month) divided by the total number of clients?

Most companies only track total revenue. If they see that revenue is going up, they think everything is okay. The reality is that revenue may be growing from net-new clients, but the revenue per client might be shrinking. If they only look at total revenue, then they will miss the opportunity to fix their cross-sell problem.

You have probably heard the old saying, "Manage the pennies and the dollars will take care of themselves." I propose that if you manage your number of clients and revenue per client, then the total revenue number will take care of itself.

If you want exponential revenue growth, then track the two revenue drivers. Put them on the wall. Discuss them at your management meetings.

Ideal Client Metrics

How well are you doing at landing and expanding inside your ideal clients? These two metrics will let you know exactly how you are doing.

Market Penetration: This measures the percentage of ideal prospects that are your clients. If there are 1,000 ideal clients in your market area and you work with 200 of them, you have 20 percent penetration of your ideal client market.

Account Penetration: This is a measurement of what percentage of your ideal clients are using each of your product or service offerings. For example, let's say that you have 100 ideal clients that can buy three categories of products that you offer. All of the clients have your core product, so you have 100 percent penetration for that product. Fifty of the clients have bought your second product category, so you have 50 percent penetration. Twenty of your clients have purchased your third category, so you have 20 percent penetration.

This account penetration dashboard shows you how well you are doing in each of your core product or service categories.

Leading Indicators

Behind the actual score of a football game, analysts track all kinds of leading indicators. Statistics like the number of first downs, yards per carry, pass completion percentage, and quarterback efficiency give us an idea of how the team is performing.

Smart teams pay attention to the leading indicators. Even if they are winning games, when a statistic like quarterback efficiency starts going backwards, something needs to be done to remedy the problem or, eventually, the team may stop winning. Data shows the teams where to focus their efforts for improvement.

You need to look at marketing and sales in the same way.

Here are some leading indicators:

100 Percent Coverage: This evaluation measures what percentage of your ideal prospects have heard from your company through marketing and sales in a given period of time.

When you created your strategy, you decided how often marketing and sales would touch key decision-makers and influencers in your ideal prospects. If you decided that they would hear from marketing at least once a month and sales at least once a quarter, then that's your standard.

Outbound Sales Coverage: Let's say you have 1,000 ideal prospects with three decision-makers for each prospect. That's 3,000 contacts. Last quarter, the sales team reached out to 1,500 of them. You now have 50 percent coverage.

Outbound Marketing Coverage: Let's say your marketing team has a goal of touching each of the 3,000 contacts with a valuable insight at least once a month. A quick search of the marketing automation system should show how many of your ideal prospect contacts did not receive at least three messages in the past 90 days. If 300 of your 3,000 contacts did not receive an email, direct mail, or social media message during that period, then you have 90 percent coverage.

100 Percent Engagement: This evaluation measures what percentage of your ideal clients are hearing from your company during a given period of time.

When you created your strategy, you decided how often marketing and sales would engage with your current ideal clients. You may have decided that sales would do a quarterly business review, while marketing would send monthly emails with valuable information to the client base.

Sales Engagement: Let's say you have 100 ideal clients. Your goal is to do a quarterly business review with each client. Last quarter, your sales team did 30. Your sales client management is 30 percent. You have a problem to fix.

Marketing Engagement: Let's say that you have a goal of monthly messages by email, direct mail, or social media to the three core decision-makers in each of your 100 ideal clients. A quick search of the marketing automation system revealed that 70 of the clients received a communication. You have 70 percent marketing engagement. You know what the problem is that needs to be fixed.

These four leading indicators should always be at 100 percent. If not, you have a problem to address. The good news is that you now know what problem needs to be fixed.

Sales may complain, saying, "I can't force a client to meet with me quarterly for our business review." That may be true, but your reps can prepare the review and send it to the client by direct mail or email.

Marketing may push back saying, "Our emails are getting blocked at some of the target companies!" That is probably true. Fortunately, you can also reach out by direct mail or social media. Marketing's job is to make sure that the message gets sent and is received.

Manage Activity, Coach Effectiveness

Leading indicators should be activity-based, not results-based. Too often, we measure results instead of activity. For example, we measure marketing by leads and salespeople by appointments. These are results, not activity.

251

Darrell Amy

Activity can be managed. Either it is getting done or it is not. If the activity is not getting done, then management needs to solve the problem.

Effectiveness is different. Your reps may have 100 percent coverage of ideal prospects, but cannot seem to get appointments. That can be coached.

Your marketing team may have 100 percent engagement with your ideal clients, but only a handful of people read the emails or show up to the educational webinars that you host. Guess what, you have an effectiveness problem. That too can be coached.

Effectiveness Metrics

To stay with our football analogy, every football team tracks more data than just the score. For offense, they track quarterback efficiency. They measure things like yards per pass, yards per carry, and yards after a reception. On defense, they measure rushing yards allowed, passing yards allowed, sacks, and tackles for loss.

Your Revenue Growth Engine has many effectiveness metrics for both marketing and sales. You should track metrics that are meaningful to your plan.

Sales Effectiveness

- Call-to-Appointment Ratio

- Appointment-to-Proposal Ratio

- Closing Ratio

- Cross-sell Percentage

Marketing Effectiveness

- Email Open Rates

- Ad Click-Throughs

- Landing Page Conversion

- Social Media Engagement

- Event Attendance

- Website Visits from Ideal Prospects

There are many more effectiveness indicators that you could track. The key is to not have so many that it just becomes noise. Choose a meaningful effectiveness indicator for each of your core marketing and sales processes. Track these and look for ways to make marginal gains in your effectiveness. As you do, you will see your engine grow.

Important Points

1. Most companies only track total revenue. If they see that revenue is going up, they think everything is okay. The reality is that revenue may be growing from net-new clients, but the revenue per client might be shrinking. If they only look at total revenue, then they will miss the opportunity to fix their cross-sell problem.

2. If you want exponential revenue growth, then track the two revenue drivers. Put them on the wall. Discuss them at your management meetings.

3. How well are you doing at landing and expanding inside your ideal clients? Marketing and account metrics will let you know exactly how you are doing.

4. Smart teams pay attention to the leading indicators. Data shows the teams where to focus their efforts for improvement.

5. Choose a meaningful effectiveness indicator for each of your core marketing and sales processes. Track these and look for ways to make marginal gains in your effectiveness.

Chapter 15: Plan and Execute

As we come to the close of this book, it is time to build your plan and execute. Tom Peters, the guru of business excellence, firmly believes that, "The thing that keeps a business ahead of the competition is excellence in execution." If you want to beat the competition, then you need to be consistent in executing your plan.

Before you can build a plan, you need to know where you are now. At the end of each chapter, there is a series of questions to help you analyze the current state of your Revenue Growth Engine.

When I conduct a Revenue Growth Workshop with a company, we begin by analyzing the current state of each cylinder of the growth engine. Our goals are to:

1. Identify Gaps: Which cylinders of the growth engine are functioning poorly?

2. Identify Low-Hanging Fruit: Where are the areas that could yield the biggest returns with the smallest investment?

The gaps and the low-hanging fruit are then listed in order of priority. This forms the basis of the plan.

255

One of the side benefits of this discussion is that it begins the process of aligning the executive, sales, and marketing leadership.

At a recent workshop, the owner of the company told our team that he was busy and could only be a part of the first few hours of the workshop where we discussed growth goals. At 5:00 p.m. that afternoon, he was still in the room, having rescheduled all his other appointments that day. Later, he told me that he learned things about his company during for that day that he was not aware of. Getting all the leadership in the room to analyze the growth engine can be very powerful.

During this process, I encourage you not to get stuck in the weeds of data analysis. While there is plenty of data available, try to keep the discussion high-level at this point. As much as you are looking for gaps, a vital outcome of this process is alignment between sales and marketing. It is important to get everyone on the same page with the gaps and low-hanging fruit. This alignment will drive the execution.

Build Your Revenue Growth Plan

Your Revenue Growth Plan is a detailed roadmap for how you will hit your company's revenue goals. It details the marketing and sales enablement plan to ensure that all cylinders of your Revenue Growth Engine are fueled and operating at peak performance.

The following is an outline of a Revenue Growth Plan we use during our workshops. You can use this model to build your own plan.

1. Get Clarity on Your Current State

Every plan begins with a benchmark of the current state. Write down these two numbers:

- **Net-new Clients**: This is the total number of clients.

- **Cross-sell Revenue**: This is the average revenue per client.

These are the two numbers you'll track over time. It is important to keep them front and center since the ultimate goal of all this activity (and work!) is to grow revenue.

2. Calculate the 10-Year Value of Ideal Clients

Next, you need to calculate the 10-year value of an ideal client. If this client bought everything that you sold, how much revenue would you realize over the next decade?

As discussed earlier in the Ideal Client chapter, 10 years is a good horizon because it helps you understand the true value of an ideal client. Building and maintaining your Revenue Growth Engine will take a lot of work and a substantial amount of resources. As you embark on this journey, you need to understand what you are aiming towards.

Understanding the lifetime value of your clients helps you make better decisions as a team. It also provides insight you can use to compare your investment of time and money to determine the true ROI.

While you are at it, go ahead and calculate the 10-year value of an average client. This should quickly put things into perspective, helping you remember the importance of focusing on ideal clients.

3. Document Your Ideal Client

Next, you need to document your ideal client. Think about this from two perspectives: tangible and intangible. Tangible items include account demographics such as company size, industry, and location.

Intangible items include the reasons you enjoy working with these clients. These could be things like:

- They are able to buy everything that we sell.

- They see us as more of a partner than a vendor.

- They value our advice.

- Our team enjoys working with them.

- They are happy to give us references.

- They pay their bills on time.

Write down as many of these characteristics as possible.

Next, identify the key decision-makers and influencers in these accounts. List the positions that are typically involved in the buying process.

4. Analyze Your Message

Now that you know who your ideal clients are, you need to consider how well your message addresses their needs. What business outcomes do your ideal clients want? Look at this through a company level first. Then, consider this at the level of each key decision-maker and influencer.

Based on your knowledge of the market, list as many of these outcomes as possible. Now, look at your message on your website, social media, sales collateral, presentations, and proposals. Do your best to read the content on these pages through the eyes of an ideal client. Does the content address the outcomes that your ideal clients want? If not, where are the gaps?

5. Map Your Ideal Prospect and Client Experience

Next, turn your attention to your prospect and client experience. Once someone engages with your company, what are the stages of the buying process? What happens once someone says "Yes" and becomes a client? These are the stages of your ideal prospect and client experience.

At each stage, think about two things. First, what is the prospect or client thinking? For example, if your first meeting is an exploratory meeting, the prospect might be thinking things like, "Will this be a waste of my time?" or "I wonder if this company is credible." After making a purchase, during the onboarding stage, the new client may have buyer's remorse and be wondering if they made a bad decision.

In addition to considering what your prospect or client might be thinking at each stage, think about what results you would like at each stage. For example, at the exploratory stage, your desired results might include the prospect being excited about moving to the next step in your process. It might also include them beginning to trust you and see the value that your team provides.

As a team, look at each stage of your buyer experience and client experience. Do this through the eyes of your ideal client. This map will be used to guide you as you improve each stage of your ideal prospect and client experience.

6. Rate Your Sales and Marketing Processes

You have looked at your message and your ideal client experience. The last step of the planning process is to evaluate your marketing and sales processes. How effective are your processes at attracting, landing, and growing ideal clients? Your Revenue Growth Engine should have processes in each of the quadrants we discussed in the earlier chapters:

- Net-New

    o Outbound Marketing

    o Outbound Selling

- Cross-Sell

    o Client Management

    o Client Communication

List your current processes in each category. Identify any additional ones that you feel are needed. For ideas, refer back to the earlier chapters in this book.

7. Set Your Priorities

Now it is time to set the priorities. This will guide the order in which you work on improving your Revenue Growth Engine. Work together as a management team to decide which items have the highest urgency and/or the potential for the fastest return.

Having been part of many of these meetings, I can predict what will happen. Your team will see the list and say, "Yes, we need all of these—right away! Let's get to work!" Overwhelmed with an impossible project, however, everyone will go back to business as usual and nothing will get done.

Begin this meeting by reinforcing that the plan you are making will roll out over the next 12–24 months. The work will take resources of time and money. It is important that each of these projects is completed with excellence.

Really, what you're embarking on is a journey to create a culture of supporting growth. This is more than just completing some projects. It is about making a commitment to build and continually fine-tune your Revenue Growth Engine. As such, this is not a short-term initiative; it is a cultural change. As the management guru Peter Drucker famously said, "Culture eats strategy for breakfast!"

This will happen over time. Set your priorities. Then, use these priorities to influence your annual plan.

8. Build an Annual Plan

Now it is time to build a plan. There are three components to executing a marketing and sales enablement plan: ongoing deliverables, campaigns, and development projects. These can be organized into a quarterly plan.

I like to organize these into a table with the next four quarters in each column. That way, as you complete one quarter, you can add a new quarter to the end. In the rows, put the activities that you're committing to do in each quarter. Let's explore each of these.

Ongoing Deliverables

Ongoing deliverables are things that never stop. Things like social media management, blogging, and search engine optimization need to happen on an ongoing basis. As you, your team, and your partners work together to complete the campaigns and projects below, it's important that this foundational work continues. That's why I recommend that you put these at the top of your list.

Campaigns

Communicating consistently with your client base requires that you continually refresh your campaigns. Set a goal to build a cross-sell bundle for your core cross-sell audiences each quarter. Build and execute a communication strategy for these. From a practical standpoint, it is a good idea to always be building 90 days ahead of when you plan to execute. For example, if you want to launch a cross-sell campaign in Q3, then build it during the summer. This gives you the time to ensure it is executed with excellence, making sure that sales and management understand the campaign and are aligned to respond to client questions.

Development Projects

Earlier, we explored the fact that your website and other marketing materials are living documents. Like an HGTV show, your digital and print collateral should be consistently renovated. Set a goal to renovate your collateral over a two-year period. Then, divide the work up over the next eight quarters. Let's say your website has a home page and seven main sections. Start with the home page in the first quarter and then move through the website, enhancing a different section each quarter. You can do the same for your print collateral. The nice thing about this strategy is that it can be agile. Let's say you launch a new product or service category. Just insert that into your quarterly project schedule and simply push the rest of the renovation ahead one quarter.

Assign the Work

Now that you've built your quarterly plan, you need to make sure that you have the resources allocated to get it done. At this point, you can work with your staff or partners to determine who will accomplish what parts of your plan.

I recommend writing up mini-statements of work for each campaign and project. This way, your employees and partners know exactly what you expect. The statement of work can contain:

1. Goals for the project

2. Dates

3. Deliverables (be specific!)

4. What a great result looks like

5. Content direction

   - Who is the target audience?

   - Key "talking points" for the outcomes you want communicated in the message

6. Design direction

Meet with your team members and partners to discuss the statement of work to make sure they are clear on the deliverables. This will ensure you get the results you want on time.

This process works well for ongoing deliverables as well. Create a statement of work for things like blogging, social media management, and search engine optimization. Itemize the specific deliverables for each month or quarter. This ensures that you, your team, and your partners are on the same page.

Quarterly Cadence

At the end of each quarter, it is time to reflect on the previous quarter and plan for the next one. During this meeting, you'll analyze your results and review your progress toward the plan. On your annual planning table, you'll delete the previous column of projects and add a new column to the end of the chart.

Plan on having your marketing and sales leadership in this meeting. This is a "roll up your sleeves" meeting where you'll invest several hours improving your growth engine.

> This is a "roll up your sleeves" meeting where you'll invest several hours improving your growth engine.

Begin the meeting by having everyone share some good news from the previous quarter. Tell success stories about what's working. I learned this from Gino Wickman, author of *Traction: Get a Grip on Your Business*. He advocates beginning each meeting by setting the tone with some positive good news.

Next, review your progress toward your goals. Show the high-level metrics: how many new clients did we add and what was our revenue per client?

Now it is time for the scorecard. Come prepared with data. Show the trends for each key metric in your Revenue Growth Engine. Identify areas where you are progressing and areas that need focus.

Then, analyze your message. Take a look at a piece of website content that's performing well, such as a page that's generating a lot of traffic with a lower-than-average bounce rate. What's working? What can you learn? Do the same for a handful of social media posts that received the most engagement and paid ads that yielded the most clicks. Finally, pull out one of your pieces of sales collateral and look at it through the eyes of a prospect or client. What could you improve?

Next, do some deal analysis together. Use the model in the previous chapter to look at some deals you won. What can you learn? Also, look at a deal that you lost. Use the lessons to inform your content and strategy.

Finally, finalize your plan for the following quarter. What processes need to be built? What area of the ideal client experience needs to be improved? What part of your message will you enhance on your website or sales collateral? What campaigns do you want to run? Who will do the work?

Write up this project plan and share it with all the parties involved. Set milestones or deadlines for each week of the quarter to keep your project on track. I also recommend that you present it in a sales meeting, so the team knows what's being done to support their success.

Weekly Marketing and Sales Alignment Meetings

Stay on track and keep alignment with a standing weekly meeting that includes your marketing and sales leader. The goals of this meeting are to stay on course with your plan and to gather input from marketing and sales on the content that needs to be created.

In this meeting, look at the quarterly plan. What milestones need to be completed this week? Spend the bulk of the meeting working on these milestones, using the time as a brainstorming session for the projects. This will ensure that both marketing and sales have input on the projects.

For example, let's say that your milestone is to create a video to be used during the onboarding phase of your client experience. Work together to decide on the purpose of the video, the key points of the script, and who will be in the video. If your milestone is a new slide deck for sales to use during a periodic business review, brainstorm the key points for the meeting.

A standing meeting each week between the sales and marketing leaders will not only ensure that projects are finished, it also gives everyone input. Best of all, sales and marketing will be in the loop on everything that is being completed.

It is Time to Get Growing!

Now it is time to grow! Simply reading this book and putting it on your shelf is not enough. I want to challenge you to take action.

My goal is to help 10,000 great businesses double their revenue. If you have a business that is dedicated to creating a great corporate culture and committed to investing in your community, I want you to grow! The world *needs* you to grow! Pulling off the plans in this book will take commitment and sustained effort. That shouldn't be a problem for you. After all, great businesses are committed to excellence. Great businesses are not afraid of hard work.

So, how can you get started? First, I recommend you share this book with your team. Buy everyone a copy or download the first two chapters and send it to them. (You can download the first two chapters for free at **www.RevenueGrowthEngine.net**)

Next, schedule a Revenue Growth Engine workshop with your team. You can find these two-day workshops in locations around the country. Our team of certified Revenue Growth Engine Implementers would be happy to facilitate one at your company. You can find these at **www.RevenueGrowthEngine.net/implementers**

From the bottom of my heart, I want you to take action. Once you do, you'll not only make a difference for yourself and your company, you'll also make a better place for your employees and their community. In exchange, all I ask is that you reinvest your growth into a non-profit organization that will make the world a better place. Imagine with me what will happen when 10,000 businesses inject millions of dollars into the non-profits that deserve our investment!

This is exciting! Let's get growing!

Resources

Congratulations on finishing this book. Now it is time to take action. As I like to say, "Let's get growing!" To help you accelerate your growth, I have put together the following resources.

Free Tool Kit

Throughout the book, you saw helpful tools that you can download for free. To save you time, I've put them all on one page that you can access here:

www.RevenueGrowthEngine.net/free-tool-kit

Free Revenue Growth Engine Discovery

Would you like to get your team on the same page? Meet with one of our certified Revenue Growth Engine Implementers. Your team will get an overview of the Revenue Growth Engine framework along with examples of how companies similar to yours are growing. We will discuss your company goals. You'll learn about two ways that you can build your engine. Learn more here. **www.RevenueGrowthEngine.net**

Book a Speaker

Would you like to motivate your audience to accelerate their revenue growth? Darrell Amy brings energy, excitement, and practical ideas to audiences of business owners, marketing professionals, and sales leaders. Learn more about how to book Darrell for your upcoming conference: **www.RevenueGrowthEngine.net/speaking**

More Resources

If you have a great company, I want to help you grow. Here are some resources you'll find helpful. While you're on the website, make sure to sign up to get updates when we add new content.

- Revenue Growth Podcast:
  www.RevenueGrowthPodcast.com

- Revenue Growth Blog:
  www.RevenueGrowthEngine.net/blog

- Favorite Revenue Growth Books:
  www.RevenueGrowthEngine.net/favorite-books

About Darrell Amy

Darrell Amy is a growth architect and is passionate about helping great companies and people grow. He is a blogger, professional speaker, and podcaster and was recently nominated to the Forbes Business Council. He is also a consultant with the C-Suite Network Advisors team.

Always learning, Darrell continues to innovate, developing new strategies for companies to grow. He regularly interacts with marketing and sales thought leaders on the *Revenue Growth Podcast* and the *Selling From the Heart Podcast.*

His ideas are firmly grounded in practical experience. After beginning his career in sales and sales management in the highly competitive office equipment business, he began helping office equipment dealers train their sales teams and develop marketing and sales plans.

In 2004, Darrell launched Convergo, a digital marketing agency that evolved from being a website development company to a complete digital marketing services agency. Through that experience, he had the opportunity to work with hundreds of small businesses, helping them develop and execute marketing plans. Today, the agency has evolved to help companies implement revenue growth strategies. As the Chief Innovation Officer at Convergo, he regularly interacts with leadership teams.

In the sales space, Darrell has trained thousands of solutions salespeople across North America, Australia, and the UK. He has helped Fortune 500 companies develop and deploy sales training programs. Today, he continues in the sales training space as a partner in Selling From the Heart, a sales training company that helps companies to integrate authenticity into every aspect of the sales process.

Darrell is actively involved in the non-profit world. He serves on the board of the Kingdom Missions Fund, a non-profit that finds and funds innovative Christian missions projects. Darrell also helps lead the ManAlive EXPEDITION, an organization focused on helping men recover their hearts and find their calling.

When he is not helping companies or people grow, you will either find him in his shop or on the water. Following in the footsteps of his father, Darrell enjoys woodworking. He loves anything on the water, including sailing and canoeing.

Darrell was born and raised in Ontario, Canada. He now lives in the southern United States on the edge of the Ozark Mountains with his sweet wife, three children, and a growing list of grandchildren.

End Notes

---

[i] Fergal Glynn, "It takes 6 to 8 Touches to Generate a Viable Sales Lead. Here's Why," https://www.salesforce.com/blog/2015/04/takes-6-8-touches-generate-viable-sales-lead-heres-why-gp.html, (April 16, 2015).

[ii] B. Joseph Pine II and James H. Gilmore. "Welcome to the Experience Economy." *Harvard Business Review*. July 1, 1998.

[iii] While talking about the buyer's journey is a vogue marketing concept these days, the concept of a buying process actually goes back almost 100 years to the functional psychologist John Dewey, who first introduced the stages of the buying process. Interestingly, the stages we use today are very similar.

[iv] Theodore Levitt, *Marketing Myopia* (Boston: Harvard Business Press, 2008).

[v] Simon Sinek, TED Talk, https://www.ted.com/talks/simon_sinek_how_great_leaders_inspire_action.

[vi] Clayton M. Christensen, Scott Cook, and Taddy Hall. "Marketing Malpractice." *Harvard Business Review*, December 2005.

[vii] James C. Anderson, James A. Narus, and Wouter Van

Rossum. "Customer value Propositions in Business Markets." *Harvard Business Review*, March 2006.

viii For more insight on how to craft a message that positions your prospects and clients as the hero, I highly recommend you check out Donald Miller's book, *Building a StoryBrand: Clarify Your Message So Customers Will Listen.*

ix Mike Schultz and John Doerr, *Insight Selling: Surprising Research on What Sales Winners Do Differently* (Hoboken, New Jersey: John Wiley & Sons, 2014).

xi It Takes 6 to 8 Touches to Generate a Viable Sales Lead.

xii Making the Case for Teleprospecting, Sirius Decisions, 2012

xiii See: https://affiliates.clickfunnels.com/affiliate-access/383c3143034

xiv Gino Wickman, *Traction: Get a Grip on Your Business* (Dallas, TX: BenBella Books, 2011).

xv Stephen R. Covey, *The 7 Habits of Highly Effective People* (New York: Free Press, 2004).

Printed in Great Britain
by Amazon

71542821R00169